My Journey Through Creationism

Can We Really Trust Evolution?

BOOK TWO

Nicholas Berardo

Kingdom Publishers

My Journey Through Creationism
Can We Really Trust Evolution? (Book Two)
Copyright© Nicholas Berardo

All rights reserved. No part of this book may be reproduced in any form by photocopying or any electronic or mechanical means, including information storage or retrieval systems, without permission in writing from both the copyright owner and the publisher of the book. The right of Nicholas Berardo to be identified as the author of this work has been asserted by him in accordance with the Copyright, Designs and Patents Act 1988 and any subsequent amendments thereto.
A catalogue record for this book is available from the British Library.
All Scripture Quotations have been taken from the New International Version and the King James Version of the Bible.

ISBN: 978-1-911697-25-1

1st Edition by Kingdom Publishers

Kingdom Publishers
London, UK.

You can purchase copies of this book from any leading bookstore or email **contact@kingdompublishers.co.uk**

Dedication

To the creationists, scientists, paleontologists, doctors without their fine research I could not have written this book.

Contents

Dedication	5
Introduction	9
Dinosaurs, Fishes, Horses, Birds	20
Entropy	57
The Flood	63
DNA	80
Good Mutations for Evolution	106
Trilobites	167
Bibliography	202

Introduction

My Journey Through Creationism
Can We Really Trust Evolution?

How Perfect God's word is
*'The Words of the Lord
Are Pure Words'*
Psalm 12:6

I would like to invite you into my journey through creation, and how, what and why these subjects related to it, intrigues me. Around September 2015, I'm on duty, though I shouldn't be watching the tablet, then on YouTube I'm watching Christian videos, not sure what, then automatically comes this debate Kent Hovind vs Jim Strayer and two other gentlemen, not sure of where the video was, but it was in one of the universities in the US.

So, I'm watching and Kent Hovind gave a brilliant speech on carbon dating, explaining how precarious the system is, well we will get into more detail into the processes of carbon dating, the methods, opinions and technology used in the system. It is thereafter, I'm watching several more creation debates with evolutionists/atheists.

I think the subject of creation is important, though it entails a lot of scientific information which some church goers, Christians may feel that they don't have much interest, because it can be too technical, tedious, and what they want to hear is Jesus and prophets and what the bible is says.

Though bearing this in mind, as you are reading, and well aware there are several scriptures in the bible that pertain to the subjects of creation. For example; Romans 12:1, this scripture is referred to as a scientific worship, and a book written by Thomas Torrance explains more about this.

You will as you go through this book, we will examine scriptures, the scientists, paleontologists, chemists, archeologists, Christians, doctors, dendrochronologists, evolutionists, astronomers, physicists and so many more what they have to comment on these fascinating topics,

I began to read the bible, seriously around 2006. Though I was not a church goer then, and none of my family was, I took, I think an ESV bible and started to read from Genesis and used highlighters through reading. The first Christian shop I visited was the Wesley Owen in Croydon, then it really took off from there. My interest in Christianity strengthened and I became more into the 'grapevine', and eventually I found that Jesus is the way and the truth.

After, months of my bible reading, and then I found there were more versions of the bible, and then I started to read them, my name Nicholas Dino Berardo, I had an Italian father and my mother from South Africa, both deceased, my father atheist, though when I was younger, I mean going back to the seventies, my father use to take us out to visit cathedrals, churches, all over the UK. My mother towards the end of her life, had a lady friend who did bible study with her. I also have a brother who also had not much interest in Christianity, that's up until now, you never know he might one day get converted. It is in Matthew 28, go and make disciples of all nations, not just converts, but disciples.

So from 2006, I'm taking Christianity seriously, though several churches around, I'm not sure which one or ones to attend. Praise god, I'm still believing and sticking to the word, I then, shortly after my mother's death, attend the All Saints in Carshalton,

Sunday mornings, I'm going there for up to a year. I then attended a church in Wallington, a big church, remember I'm living in Waddon, Croydon then, I went there for about 6 months, and then to another Anglican church in Wallington.

Now I'm going around like a 'free agent' not sure of what church I should settle in. Problem also being that these Sundays, which I had to get booked off, as I work as a security officer, I'm asked to work on most Sundays. Eventually I found the church, Metropolitan Tabernacle, Elephant & Castle, Dr. Peter Masters giving great teaching. I had attended Hillsong, and KT Notting Hill, so many churches of various denominations, so one is bound to find what he or she is looking for, Psalm 133:1, How pleasant it is how brethren dwell together in unity, and of course Hebrews 10:25 the assembling of ourselves in meeting together.

I was born on 2nd June 1966, I attended a church school, I think around 1970 to 1971, near Kirkdale. Sydenham, SE26 (St. Philip's School). Then Langbourne Primary School.Dulwich 1972 to 1977. Kingsdale School 1977 to 1984. There on I went to college, studied Illustration/Graphics for 3 years and worked as a technical illustrator from 1989 to 1991. I was then made redundant by two companies! Really had to consider a career change, being unemployed and still sending my CV to employers/agencies. I had a BTEC National Diploma in Illustration, City Guilds in Illustration in 1987 to 1988. From 1992 to 1994 abouts, I did three part time courses, IT training, City and Guilds, A Library course that was a City and Guilds for a year, and an RSA stage 2 in IT in 1994. Though, I pushed myself in trying to pursue a career within this training, nothing materialized, and as my money situation was bleak, I'm now having to work in security up until now.

It was on some day not sure the exact date in 2010, I met some young guy, who was preaching out loud by the brow of the hill, where the tram travels, just opposite of the side of the Primark. I really thank the lord I had met this street evangelist, Hebrews 13:5 Never will I leave you, Never will I forsake you. It is my encounter with this evangelist that really 'pushed' me into Christianity. Thereon after, we started going round various parts of London, Walthamstow, Tottenham, Seven Sisters, Evangelism, Bible Study, Meetings. I was then a few years after, I got baptised, speaking in tongues. I got more involved with more Christians, fellowship, dinners, singing, church, though, it wasn't all plain sailing we would meet people who were facing problems. Jeremiah 29: 12-14, Then will you call upon me and go and pray to me, and I will listen to you'.

So, go ahead and pick up that bible today, and get into the word. Kent Hovind would say it's not time to get worried, but time to get busy. While, some twiddling their thumbs, scratching our heads, the answers are there in the bible. Like Job, who suffered tremendously, Job kept on asking questions to the lord and then soon found that his questions/prayers were answered Job 38, the Lord from a storm answered. Therefore, how much torment, suffering we endure, the lord will answer. Trust in God alone, Proverbs 3:5 Trust in the Lord, and lean not on your own understanding.'

Now, getting back to what I said originally about creation. I am a believer in the creation of everything, from the last 6 to 10,000 years. As you read through this book, I shall provide evidence, data, theories, testimonies how god created everything. Isaiah 55:8, Our ways, thoughts are not the Lord's ways thoughts, we have to appreciate how God's perfection is all around us.

The atheist might say, well if god is so good, why do we have all the disease, famine, suffering, wickedness, disasters, catastrophes all around us. God has given mankind freewill, though they say, there is this all-powerful being, is responsible? Well, we can go with several scriptures saying, why when, how god is explaining to the unbeliever, agnostic.atheist. 1 Peter 1:23, been born again not of corruptible, but of incorruptible seed. I have to say that evolutionists, their view of life is pretty damning. I mean if I had to believe that when we die that our final is in that coffin. It just seems so futile, no wonder we have so many suicide, drug related issues that people face no hope at all.

Take for example, Bill Nye, the science guy. When he was with Ken Ham at his exhibit, Ham askes Nye what happens when we die. Nye replies 'Our genes are passed on' Well, at least he says our genes are passed on, so maybe by what he says, he has hope? I only pray that he comes to Christ. John 17:3 'And this life is eternal'.

Cancer, sickness, disease, people with handicap, deaf, blind, well God certainly doesn't take kindly to this. Genesis 3:17, 'Cursed is the ground for thy sake'. Though, some have difficulty as Adam sinned humans are subject to suffering. Psalm 103:1-4 ':Lord forgives all your sins and heals all your diseases'. All of us have sinned and no one does what is righteous and never sins. Ecclesiastes 7:20, 1 John 1:8 'If we say we never sinned we deceive ourselves'

Jeremiah 30:17: I will restore your health, and heal your wounds' the miracles are there, and miracle workers, the ones that passed away, rest assured Isaiah 57: 'The righteous are taken away, they enter peace, they find rest and lie in death.

If I had to believe what some evolutionists view on life is quite damning. If when we die, we go into a coffin and or be cremated.

Isaiah 55:8, KJV 'For my thoughts are not your thoughts., neither your ways are my ways, and my thoughts than your thoughts.

So this is what I intended to write about, important to myself and everybody, this is what I think, and you should give some consideration.

So what do we mean about creation and evolution? How can we be sure which is the more accurate, truthful verifiable, say. Well, this has to be researched to some degree, though, in one topic, say in the formation of stars, evolution would give one account, say the big bang, and creation would give another. As Christians we have the young earth creationists and the old earth creationists. I believe that God's word is the most accurate and concise.of any written word since time began.

Can we say that we are still complying to God's word, when the book of Genesis says that everything was created in the last 6 to 10,000 years. Or, can we accept that everything was made in the last 200,000 years. The famous Canadian Hugh Ross, maintains that everything was created in a greater period than 10,000 years, and he has written some books on it. On some of his theories, he bases it on Isaiah 42:5, stretching of the heavens. Isaiah 45:12, and Psalm 104:2, all these scriptures are using the verb stretching the heavens. So Ross, puts emphasis on these scriptures and on some others, to confirm his ideas, that the universe is expanding.

Though, we have to examine these ideas, and other evolutionary theses, and to see if they stand up to real scrutiny. I make the first chapter, that is the universe this eternal space full of vast amounts of stars, planets, comets meteors, to see how the Christian faith has with scriptures has brought us to believe that god is real, and how the atheistic, agnostics has explained against the God of creationism. So, I will outline the reasons backed by creationists, chemists, doctors anthropologists, paleontologists.

There are many ways we can go about this, the evidence, facts, data information, possible eye-witness accounts, then maybe, we could all have an answer, we would all love something like that.

Colossians 1:16 KJV'

'For by him were all things created, that are in heaven, and that are in earth, visible and invisible, 'whether they be thrones, or dominions, or principalities, or powers. All things were created by him and for him.'

The Big Bang theory. Does the theory have any harmony or truth to it all? Are we to believe that this was caused by an infinitesimal tiny mass that exploded, or expanded, as which some scientists do believe. Let's also consider that they could not come with a definite time when it originated.

The list below are the years that scientists changed when this big bang supposedly happened, as I mentioned above by Kent Hovind in his creation speech;

1954

1960

1966

1970

1974

The Big Bang time that it occurred was contradicted more than five times., if not probably more,

Then we have to take into account the stars, constellations, formation of galaxies, the vast numbers of them. The atheists are saying how could God have created all this in 10,000 years.

Psalm 131:1 KJV,

"LORD, my heart is not haughty, nor my eyes lofty: neither do I exercise myself in great matters, or in things too high for me".

In the KJV translation the 'heaven' is written in singular, whereas the other versions have it as plural.

The stars Psalm 147:4 KJV;

'He telleth the number of stars; he calleth all by their names'. The atheists are saying how can god name all the stars? According to one doctor, if the universe is 13.7 billion years old as the Big-Bang theory suggests, it would take 1 million stars per second to count them all.

In my first chapter, I will mention the brilliant men and women who during their time of research, the limited resources facilities, their calculations, conclusions, predictions they were to come up with.

Was Georges Lemaitre the Belgian priest right in his theory that the universe came from a dot of nothing. The Higgs' Mass theory states that the dot of nothing occurred 10 -32 secs, before the beginning. The Electro Weak Era.

Genesis 1:1 KJV;

'In the beginning, God created heaven, and the earth'.

If you saw a car, you know when you saw it (time) beginning.
You know where you saw the car (space) heaven.
You know what you saw the car (earth) matter

These three statements have to come together simultaneously as we can understand what's happening. In other words, if you saw an object (matter), and saw where the object was (heaven). If there was no time (beginning). This would be impossible, because for you to see the object there must be a time allocated to it. If you had time, and space only. This would mean complete emptiness. Matter must be in existence.

I come back to cosmology the stars, interesting scripture in Amos 5:8 KJV;

'Seek him that maketh the seven stars and Orion, and turneth the shadow of death in the morning, and maketh the day dark with night.that calleth for the waters of the sea, and poureth them out upon the face of the earth: The LORD is his name'.

Notice here the seven stars and Orion. The seven stars are specifically what?

Job 38:31 KJV;

'Canst thou bind the sweet influences of Pleiades, or the loose bands of Orion?'

Job, perhaps may have understood this, but did not have much knowledge of ordinances.

It is claimed by scientists that the estimate in the universe there is 7 sextrillion stars, that is each one of us could own 11 million stars each.

We then go to the creation of Adam, and look at 1 Corinthians 15:39 KJV;

'All the flesh, is not the same flesh: but there is one kind of flesh of men, another flesh of beasts, another kind of fish, and another for birds'.

Saying that the flesh of man is different to to that of beasts this is what one professor, Prof Von Hume said;

'If Adam was biologically a beast, into whom God breathed his spirit and thus 'humanized' him, then Adam was not the first man biologically'.

And this what Darwin said about how before living creatures were formed;

'We could conceive in some worm in a little pond with all sorts of ammonia and phosphoric salts, light, heat, and electricity, etc. that a protein compound was chemically formed ready to undergo still more complex changes. At the present day, such matter would be instantly devoured or absorbed, which would have not been the case before living creatures were formed'.

The explanation of the theory of entropy, here is one account of how a 'closed system' might have occurred.

'A system that is closed to life from the outside, arid to intelligent technique is not necessarily closed thermodynamically. Even if a system is closed, the entropy of one section or component may actually decrease, provided only that the total entropy of the system increases and an example of this might well be laboratory synthesis of highly complicated molecules from the juxtaposition of molecules that are less complex.

Bishop Ussher made calculations for Genesis 2, this was on the basis of the Masoretic text. He concluded that the flood must have happened in the third millennium BC. However, the Septuagint text interprets that the flood occurred in the 4th millennium.

The Greek philosopher Pliny Said;

'Human beings are distributed all around the earth, and stand with their feet pointing towards each other'

Here, is a quote from William Herschel in 1813 when he observed the stars;

'I have observed the stars of which the light, it can be proved, can take two million years to reach the earth'.

Fred Hoyle 'In Galaxies, Nuclei, and Quasars 1965' said this about the universe;

'There should be a difference between an anti-observer who reads the universe from the future to the past, and our ordinary procedure from reading it from past to future. This is due to the particles that can be switched by switching the sense of time'.

Some atheists might put on their graveyards, Rest In Peace RIP. Well, they believe they will be transferred to another species. Then, what would be the point in being remembered? The evolutionists still can't explain which of the species, specifically will evolve to another. Pakicetus to whale, if that's true? Ok, but what about the other millions of species?

Some atheists can't remember who, was so convinced by looking at the DNA of a chimpanzee, ape and compared it with a human, with human chromosomes 46. He claimed that they are direct ancestors.

A debate with Ken Ham and Bill Nye the science guy. Nye made the claim that when the marsupials left the Ark in Mt Ararat to Australia, he had a map to show that we should be able to find fossils in the same area, and in a straight direction. Now, how can he be certain of this, because they are marsupials that they would have all travelled in the same way. Can we not consider the possibility that some of the marsupials and others took different directions?

Chapter 1

Dinosaurs, Fishes, Horses, Birds

Fossil History of The Horse

The horse is traced from an animal of the size of a fox terrier, known as Eohippus. Through several forms which are said to represent steps in its evolutionary development to the present horse. The horse was meant to have increased in size, limbs, dentition. Eohippus had an arched back and had four toes on its front feet with three toes as remnants of two others on its hind feet. It's teeth had crowns and rough surfaces. It is supposed to have lived in the Eocene period, and later in the same period Orohippus. A larger horse. The fossils come from New Mexico, Wyoming, this gave rise to a more advanced form the Epihippus. (Ref John Klotz, Genes, Genesis and Evolution, page 187)

In the Oligocene period Mesohippus is supposed to have developed. It was 18 to 24 inches tall and had three toes on each foot. The middle toes on all four feet were the largest. Later Miohippus, a little larger but quite similar, is supposed to have evolved. In the early part of the Miocene or the lower Miocene. Parahippus is a transitional form between Miohippus and Merychippus, which followed it to the Middle Miocene period. Merychippus had long crowned fully cemented molars. It had three toes, the lateral toes never reached the ground. It was one-toed. It was followed by Protohippus in the late, Upper Miocene.

The Pliohippus in the Pliocene period. The latter is the first toed horse and was 40 inches tall. Protohippus is supposed to give rise to Hipparion in the Miocene. Pliohippus is supposed to give rise to Plesippus, which shows no trace of lateral toes. This gave rise to the modern horse, Equus which is supposed to have appeared in the Upper Pliocene period. Up to the Miocene, horses have been browsers then taken to grazing. Most horse fossils are from American rocks, few found in European formations.

Horse Series

The Horse has often been cited as an example of evolution. There are five hypothetical stages representing the geological periods from the Eocene Pleistocene. A number of objections to the view that it is an evolutionary series.

The horse species are the perissodactyls, which include rhinos tapirs the odd-toed ungulates. The even-toed ungulates, hippos, deer.

The other horses are the Dinohippus single hoofed., the Hypohippus, the Nannippus.

1./Most of the morphological characteristics of the feet, skull, and teeth, which are traditionally supposed to exhibit an almost perfect sequence of change through the Tertiary period.

2./ The most famous of all the equid trends, the gradual reduction of the side toes, cannot be traced as a sequence. The Eocene horses had padded dog-like feet with four functional toes in front and three behind. The early Oligocene and all subsequent horses are without a functional front toe and concentrate weight on the middle toe.

3./ Eohippus, is Eocene and Miocene, but its bones are found on the surface. Eohippus fossils have been found in the Eocene strata.

4./ The fossils represented show an increase in size from Eocene to the present day.

5./ Eohippus has a skeleton very similar to the present day Hyrax. (a small guinea-pig like animal). Some scientists believe that Eohippus has no connection with modern horses, it is believed to be a variant form of Hyrax.

6./The horse sequence, if indeed it shows genetic change at all, is an example of micro, rather than macro evolution. The period from the Eocene to present is supposedly 60 million years. If it took this time for minor changes in a horse, then it must have taken around ten times, to develop a new biological order, and ten times to develop a new class. This would total 6 billion years an order of magnitude longer than the 600 million years since the evolution of the Cambrian period. (Ref Colin mitchell, Case for Creationism, page 133 to 134)

In the Origin Darwin was able to point out the extinct Hipparion, the early three toed horse, as an intermediate between the existing horses and certain older five-toed forms; to the extinct Dugong Halitheriium as an intermediate between the modern Sirenia an hoofed quadrupeds, because it possessed an ossified thigh bone which articulated to a well-defined acetabulum in the pelvis; Zeuglodon, an early whale., this as a connecting link between the Carnivora and Cetacea., and the Archeopteryx.

Even Darwin was surprised when in Uruguay 180 years ago they uncovered this 'Macrauchenia patachonica' this ungulate made Darwin say

'The strangest animal discovered'. It could not be confirmed whether they were elephants, rodents.

The Hipparion seems to be the only convincing intermediate, Hipparion and modern horses are trivial as mutant horses are occasionally born with three toes today. (Ref Micheal Denton, Evolution, A Theory in Crisis, page 57, 1996)

The gap between the sea cow- Halitherium and the hoofed quadrupeds is enormous, as the gap between the primitive whale and Zeuglodon and the carnivores.

The history of the horse is traced from an animal size of a fox, known as Eohippus. Eohippus was known to have an arched back four toes on its front feet. Three toes on its hind feet. It is supposed to have lived in the Eocene period. The Megohippus was from the Oligocene period. The Mesohippus was formed 18 to 24 inches tall. It had three feet on its front and hind feet. Miohippus was larger from the Miocene period. Parahippus was the transition from Miohippus and Merychippus followed in the middle Miocene period.

The Merychippus followed by Protohippus in the upper Miocene period. The Pliohippus in the Pliocene period was a three toed horse 40 inches tall. The Protohippus was supposed to have given rise to the Hipparion in the Miocene period. Pliohippus is supposed to have given rise to Plesippus showing no trace of lateral toes. This gave rise to the modern horse Equus which is supposed to have appeared in the upper Pliocene period.

(Ref Genes Genesis Evolution John Klotz, page 187, 1955)

G.G.Simpson "The Major Features of Evolution" 1953, page 263 his comments;

'The most famous equid trends "gradual reduction of the side toes" is flatly fictitious. There was no such trend in any line of Equidae.....Eocene horses all had digitigrade padded, doglike feet with four functional toes in front and three behind. In a rapid transition (not actually represented by fossils), early Oligocene horses lost one functional front toe and concentrated weight a little more on the middle hoof as a step-off point...This type persisted without essential change in all browsing horses.'

Richard Owen "Anatomy of Vertebrates, page 795, 1866, gave the following account on the horse series;

'A modern horse occasionally come into the world with supplementary ancestral hoofs......In the latest examples, the inner splint-bone, answering to the second metacarpal of the pentadactyl foot, supported phalanges and a terminal hoof, in position and proportion to the middle hoof, resembling the corresponding one in Hipparion.

'In relation to actual horses such specimen figures as "monstra per excessum" ;but, in relation to miocene horses, they would be normal and those of the present day would exemplify "monstra per defectum". The mother of a "monstrous" tridactyle colt might repeat the anomaly and bring forth a tridactyle "filly" ; just as, at San Salvador, the parents of a family of six had two of the series boron with defective brain sand of dwarf size: they were "male" and "female" and these strange little idiots are exhibited as "Aztecs". The pairing of the horses with the metapodials bearing, according to type, phalanges and hoofs, might restore the race of hipparions'.

Fossil History of The Horse

The horse is traced from an animal of the size of a fox terrier, known as Eohippus. Through several forms which are said to represent steps in its evolutionary development to the present horse. The horse was meant to have increased in size, limbs, dentition. Eohippus had an arched back and had four toes on its front feet with three toes as remnants of two others on its hind feet. It's teeth had crowns and rough surfaces. It is supposed to have lived in the Eocene period, and later in the same period Orohippus. A larger horse. The fossils come from New Mexico, Wyoming, this gave rise to a more advanced form the Epihippus. (Ref John Klotz, Genes, Genesis and Evolution, page 187)

In the Oligocene period Mesohippus is supposed to have developed. It was 18 to 24 inches tall and had three toes on each foot. The middle toes on all four feet were the largest. Later Miohippus, a little larger but quite similar, is supposed to have evolved. In the early part of the Miocene or the lower Miocene. Parahippus is a transitional form between Miohippus and Merychippus, which followed it to the Middle Miocene period. Merychippus had long crowned fully cemented molars. It had three toes, the lateral toes never reached the ground. It was one-toed. It was followed by Protohippus in the late, Upper Miocene. The Pliohippus in the Pliocene period. The latter is the first toed horse and was 40 inches tall. Protohippus is supposed to give rise to Hipparion in the Miocene. Pliohippus is supposed to give rise to Plesippus, which shows no trace of lateral toes.. This gave rise to the modern horse, Equus which is supposed to have appeared in the Upper Pliocene period. Up to the Miocene, horses have been browsers then taken to grazing. Most horse fossils are from American rocks, few found in European formations.

For the "cursorial theory" Ostrom believed that bird flight evolved through bipedal running. His account of the cursorial theory;

'The cursorial theory postulates a sequence of stages from a primitive Quadrupedal reptile, to a facultative biped, to an obligatory cursorial biped. Followed by stages of elongation of the forelimbs and scales…….increasing "thrust" surfaces Flapping action of these "photowings" supposedly added thrust to the hindlimbs and greater acceleration. This was presumed to have led to flight velocities to al least partial conversion of the forelimbs from "propellers" into wings'

(Ref Micheal Denton, Evolution, A Theory In Crisis, pages 205-206, 1996)

Ostrom commented on the "cursorial theory";

'The cursorial theory of bird flight origins has received virtually no acceptance, apparently for several good reasons....including the seemingly impossible "bootstrap" effort required for the animal to lift itself by means of flapping proto-wings.'

It is particularly doubtful that "feathers" evolving to form an insect net would provide the basis for an impervious aerofoil. If a reptile's scale did ever evolve, it would be pervious to air and be unsuitable for any type of flight. (Ref Micheal Denton, Evolution, A theory in Crisis, pages 207-209, 1996)

Elephants

The elephant "sequence" which starts from a hypothetical ancestral form, somewhere between a modern Hyrax, (a small rodent-like rat found in Africa, via pig sized Moeritherium of the late Eocene, a series of forms showing increase in trunk size. Teeth morphology to the modern elephant does not convince, Sylvia Sikes, "The Natural History of The African Elephant" 1971, page 2;

'It requires extreme elasticity of the imagination to see anything more than a Very superficial resemblance between the available parts of the skeletons of the earliest hyraces and those of the Proboscidea.......It is apparent in the past disproportionate weight was given to skeletal affinities, while important characteristics are overlooked.....perhaps we should admit that the sitting of Moeritherium in an intermediate position in the family tree savours more of the artistic requirements of the drawing board than of the honest admission of ignorance as to its proper position'

(Ref Micheal Denton, Evolution, A Theory In Crisis, page 185, 1996)

The difference between the Eohippus and the modern horse is trivial, and the two forms are separated by sixty million years and at least ten genera, and a great number of species.

Creatures Without Ancestral Forms

The following animals, there is no evidence they had ancestral evolution.

Elephants, The lineage of elephants is thought to date back to 55 million years to the Eocene period. The earliest supposed ancestor, Palaeomastadon, had a completely formed trunk the same as that of modern elephants. Palaeomastadon is assumed to have descended from a proboscidean ancestor, but no half-trunk intermediate form is found. (Ref T.H.Tier Creation: The Only Reasonable Explanation of Natural Phenomena, 1970).

Giraffes, We now know that acquired characteristics cannot be inherited and there is no fossil evidence that giraffes have evolved from common neck ancestors. There are further reasons why the giraffe's neck cannot have evolved. Its head is a long way from its body, the giraffe requires an extra large heart to pump the blood to it's head to avoid brain damage. It has to lower it's head to drink and the very power of the heart would then risk causing an excessive blood flow to the brain. It spreads its front legs apart reducing blood pressure. Jugular veins have valves that stop blood rushing to the brain when it lowers its head.. It has a spongy tissue at the back of the brain which 'soaks up' any excess blood.

Whales, the following changes can be explained in the absence of missing links. The hind limbs became tail flukes, the pelvic bones were reduced. The forelimbs beame paddles. The suckling developed underwater. All the accompanying musculature changes occurred, and the sieve (baleen) developed in the whale's mouth. (Ref Colin Mitchell, Case for Creationism, page 135, 1994)

Sharks and Fish

Job 41:1 KJV

'Canst thou draw out the leviathan with a hook? Or his tongue with a cord, which thou lettest down?

Psalm 148:7 KJV

'Praise the Lord from the earth. Ye dragons and all deeps'

Daniel 7:3 KJV

'And four beasts came up from the sea, diverse one from another'

According to Anaximander of Miletus (550BC) one of the earliest of nature philosophers, life was generated by material processes from sea slime, an idea reminiscent of modern theories of the origin of life and the prebiotic soup. His attempt was to give a natural explanation of the origin and diversity of life. His theory was incomplete, and it failed to deal with the problem of organic design.

Empedocles (450BC) was one of the first to realize that the phenomena of adaptive complexity required a specific framework of a naturalistic scheme. His theory to account for the design of organisms preceded Darwin by two thousand years. (Ref Micheal Denton, Evolution, A Theory in Crisis, page 39, 1996)

G.G. Simpson stated;

"Half and probably two-thirds or more of the Middle Oligocene genera are known and that those not yet known are mainly carnivores (individually much less abundant than herbivores) and very small ,mammals"

Number of living orders of terrestrial vertebrates	43
Number of living orders of terrestrial vertebrates found as fossils	42
Percentage fossilised	97.7%
Number of living families of terrestrial vertebrates	329
Number of living families of terrestrial vertebrates found as fossils	261
Percentage fossilised	79.1%
Number of living families of terrestrial vertebrates found as fossils excluding birds	178
Number of terrestrial vertebrates found as fossils excluding birds	156
Percentage fossilised	87.8%

(Ref Micheal Denton, Evolution, A Theory In Crisis, pages 189-190)

Dragons, Leviathan, Behemoth

Isaiah 27:1 KJV;

'That day the LORD with his sore and great and strong sword shall punish leviathan the piercing serpent, even leviathan that crooked serpent; and he shall slay the dragon that is in the sea.'

Job 41:1 KJV;

'CANST thou draw out leviathan with a hook? Or his tongue with a cord, which thou lettest down?'

Psalm 104 25 -26 KJV

'So is this great and wide sea, wherein are things creeping innumerable, both small and great beasts. There go the ships, there is that Leviathan whom thou hast made to play therein'

The word Dragon in Hebrew 'Tannin' was a term used to symbolize the power of Egypt. Many scriptures in the bible have the term dragon. It was in 1841, Richard Owen the biolologist had given the name 'dinosaur' to these great reptiles. The term 'dinosaur' from greek translation is, terrible lizard. Coming back to the word 'Tannin' there are different meanings Tan and Tannin. Tan is used as a plural for a creature living in desert places. Evolutionists say the dinosaurs became extinct some 65 to 70 million years ago, then we have had reports/sightings of a strange large sauropod like animals in the last fifty years, one example is the mokele mbembe, In the Congo of Africa.If you saw back in the early 1980's the mysterious world programme by Arthur C. Clarke, the then professors James Powell and Roy Mackal, were on expeditions in the Congo, where the pygmies describe this animal the mokele mbembe as some sort of large brontosaurus/diplodocus type animal. They call it 'nyamala'.

Isaiah 51:9 KJV;

'Awake, awake, put on strength, O arm of the LORD; awake, as in the ancient days, in the generations of the old. Art thou not it that hath cut. Rahab and wounded the dragon?'

Micah 1:8 KJV;

'Therefore, I will wail and howl, I will go stripped and naked. I will make a wailing like the dragons, and mourning like the owls'

Isaiah 34:13 KJV;

'And thorns shall come up in her palaces, nettles and brambles. In the fortresses thereof: and it shall be a habitation of dragons and a court of owls'

Revelation 12, 13-16, has the account of a woman that was persecuted by a dragon that was cast down to earth. The woman was given wings to fly to the wilderness, there she was in the presence of a serpent that spewed out water to help her in the flood. The earth helped her and consumed the flood. The dragon was enraged with her offspring.

The Behemoth Job 40:15 According to 'The Trumpet' the behemoth was an animal 'Baluchitherium' they say it fits the description well, as it was the largest mammal ever. So what exactly is or was the Baluchitherium?

Well Wikipedia, is saying that it is of a species Paraceratherium which was an extinct giant rhinoceros that lived in the late Oligocene period around 30 million years ago. According to discovery, bones were uncovered by a palaeontologist Sir Clive Forster Cooper in 1910 in Balochistan in Pakistan, and owing to the huge size of the bones he named it 'Baluchitherium' and a further expedition was made by french palaeontology Jean Loup Welcomme who went near Balochistan Dera Bugti where Cooper found the bones.

Then what did happen to Baluchitherium? It is believed that 22 million years ago movements of Africa, Asia destroyed the 'Tethy' prehistoric sea, and in Balochistan the vegetation disappeared causing Baluchitherium to go extinct, however Welcome contacted Nawab Khan Bugti who gave further permission to Welcome to excavate, found there were more remains uncovered of Baluchitherium of both male and female.

In 2003 A french team decided that the Baluchitherium was around 5 metres tall, weighing around 20 tons. So this could be one explanation for what could have been the mighty Behemoth.

Another idea Behemoth had was that it was a Rodhocetus. This aquatic sea animal, a Rhodo Whale, came from the Eocene period 47 million years ago, being 10ft long weighing up to 1000 pounds This animal was a whale that lived on the shore. The Rodhocetus according to evolution was a whale in between the Kutchicetus and the Dorudon. The first of its ancestors would have been the hippopotamus. In another evolution theory the Rodhocetus was in between the Dalanistes and the Takracetus, and the Dorudon is listed as a further four stages of development of evolution, of another 40 million years, in the Eocene period.

We have Tiktaalik, Coelacanth, Ogopogo, Lochness Monster, countless number of sightings, photos, eye witness accounts of some strange dinosaur-like animal in these lakes/rivers. In 1977, Sandra Mansi at Lake Champlain took a very convincing photo of an animal with a serpent-like neck, it was named 'Champ'.

Though it is believed that the Tiktaalik had lived some 375 million years ago during the Devonian period, the Tiktaalik has been a recent discovery around 2004 in the Canadian Arctic. It has been said it was a cross between a fish and crocodile.

Scripture references Isaiah 13:22, 34:13, a satyr a large goat like animal, Malachi 1:3, Job 40:15, Psalm 91:13 describes a serpent like dragon. A great example in scripture from the kjv version is Job 41:1, 'Canst thou draw out a leviathan with a hook, or his tongue with a cord which thou lettest down? Canst thou put a hook into his nose, or bore his jaw with a thorn?.

How then can the Leviathan be described?. In Psalm 74:14 the Leviathan is described as a multihead creature or serpent. It is also described as having seven heads. The hebrew word for Leviathan 'leviathan' Job 41:33 NIV 'Nothing on earth is its equal a creature without fear' so this is referring that the Leviathan is one of the most awesome creatures on earth.

Another theory is that the Leviathan was a giant crocodile that was around 11 metres, the Sarcosuchus. If we then look at Job 41:13 NIV ' Who can strip off its outer coat? Who can penetrate its double coat of armour? This itself describes an animal with a tough outer skin with a coat of armour. What comes to mind the only creatures that fit this description are crocodiles. In verse 19 'Flames stream out of its mouth 'Then in verse 20 'smoke pours from its nostrils' so the animal is able to extinguish smoke.

The Leviathan is described as a huge river/ sea monster. In Job 40:17, It says 'He moveth his tail like a cedar. A Cedar tree which it seems to refer to cannot be the tail of an elephant or hippopotamus, their tails are too small to fit this description.

In the apocrypha Daniel 14 says that Daniel boiled up lumps and tossed into the dragon's mouth which then blocked its intestine. In Isaiah 51:9, the lord pierced the monster of the river Nile.

The finest of the ancient hebivorates were the mammoths and the mastodons. This rules out much larger variant forms of dinosaurs, such as the ceratopsians (horned dinosaurs) , the ornithopods (duck-billed dinosaurs) stegosaurus (plated dinosaurs) giant sauropods (87 ½ ft diplodocus).(Ref Donald Patten Biblical Flood, Ice Epoch page 233-234)

Genesis 9:20 -21

The process of fermentation, of which Noah was ignorant, and which occasioned his involuntary drunkenness was due to the climatic changes incidental to the same cause, the fall of the watery canopy that enveloped the earth. Several antelopes and other animals have been found embedded in Siberian ice with undigested grass in their stomachs, which betrays a sudden watery death immediately followed by freezing within solid ice, and the grass would have been preserved intact for over 4,300 years.

So these facts prove the reality of the deluge, and proves there was a canopy of water that enveloped the earth, and that it fell six others had fallen, composed of such solids, gases and acids to form the six great strata of rocks whose best example is the Grand canyon.

(Ref Epiphany Studies in Scripture, Series 2, creation, Paul S. Johnson page 325, 1938)

Dinosaurs

The Mesozoic era - age of the reptiles would be dinosaurs. Dinosaurs are thought to have developed from Cotylosaurs through theCodonts. The Codons are assigned to the sub-order Pseudopodia.

The dinosaurs are thought to have developed from the cotylosaurs, through the thecodonts. Crocodile reptiles that also gave rise to the pterosaurs and crocodiles. Some of the earliest and least specialized of these, supposedly from the Upper Triassic, were not much larger than roosters except for their long lizard-like tails. It is generally believed that like our modern reptiles, they were cold-blooded. The Compsognathus, it was about 2 ½ ft about the size of a cat.

The largest dinosaur recorded is the Giganotosaurus of East Africa, whose length was probably about 80ft, it is thought to have weighed about 40 tons.

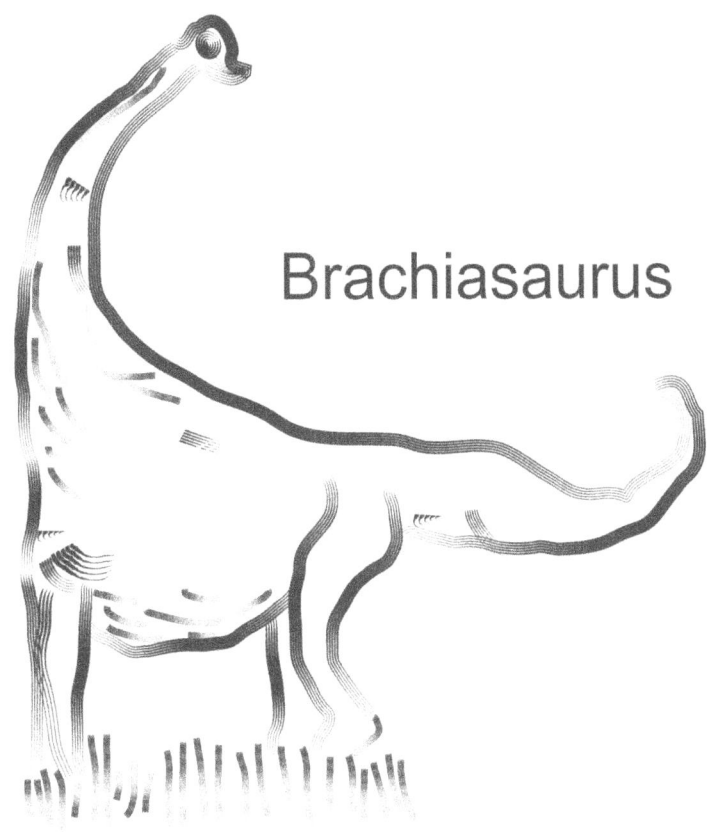

Brachiasaurus

Dinosaurs appear to have been worldwide in distribution, no dinosaur has been discovered in New Zealand. They were divided into two groups, the Saurischia, and the Ornithischia. Both of these are believed to have descended from a form similar to a swamp dwelling cotylosaur.

The earliest dinosaurs were the Saurischia. They walked on their hind legs, with a long slender tail, most of them were carnivorous. The most fearful was the Tyrannosaurus, it reached a length of 47ft and weighed about 8 to 10 tons. The head being about 4ft. Its front legs could not reach the mouth so it could not be used in feeding.

The Tyrannosaurus is placed under the suborder Carnosauria..A sauriscian suborder Coelurosauria another of the Sauropoda. The Sauropods are believed to represent evolution and went too far to become aberrant.

The Brontosaurus was about 66ft long and weighed about 38 tons. The Diplodocus 67ft had a terminal 10ft tail which was used as a whiplash for it's defence. (Ref John Klotz, Genes, Genesis and Evolution, pages 470 to 473).

The depth of silt required to bury a 10ft dinosaur would have taken 10,000 years to accumulate at deep-ocean rates. It is hard to imagine that any single fossilization process occurring at the assumed rates.

Of one foot in a 1,000. (Ref Oliver Barclay, Creation and Evolution, page 51, 1985)

Sauropods

W.D. Matthew "The Pose of Sauropods Dinosaurs" 1910, he said "Sauropods, one of the extinct lizard-like reptiles, could not walk on land" He believed that they were so heavy they would have collapsed without water to support their weight. He believed these animals lived in water at the edge of the ocean, marshes or lakes, where part of their weight was supported by buoyancy of water.

A set of fossil footprints from Barnum Brown indicated that sauropods did walk on land. (Ref John Klotz, Genes, Genesis and Evolution page 191)

The necks of Sauropod dinosaurs can be up to 15m in length, and are times longer than some giraffes. The elasmosaurid plesiosaur was different from most sauropods with short cervicals.

Sauropods believed to represent forms in which evolution went too far and became aberrant, (abnormal divergent). Sauropods were considered to be senile forms that died out before some other dinosaurs.

Brachiosaurus would be a fine example of sauropod. With its long neck around 80ft and height of 40ft.

Sauropod dinosaurs were mainly herbivorous dinosaurs. Although they were according to evolutionary stages, they were from the late Triassic to the Middle Triassic period.

It is said that any animal with a size of a giraffe's body, it would be impossible to carry a 10m long neck. It is therefore that neck length is allometric in relation to the body size of sauropods.

The hadrosaurid and the proboscidean and the indricotherium mammals were also recognized as sauropods. Richard Lydekker named these sauropds in 1893 from South America as two new species of Titanosaurus T. Australis and T. Nanus and Argyrosaurus and Microcoleus.

It is believed that the Xenoposeidon Pronenoneukos was the earliest known 'brachiosaurus' sauropod dinosaur of the Early Cretaceous period from: Michael P.Taylor Dept of Earth Sciences, University of Bristol in November 2017. A New Sauropod Dinosaur of Wealden South England.

Quadrupedally is the main feature of Sauropod dinosaurs that they walk on all fours according to one report the Sauropod dinosaurs were megaherbivores 'giant plant eaters' of 140 million years in the Mesozoic. They diversified in the middle Jurassic and developed into 120 species, accounting for one fifth as being non-avian dinosaurs.

Ornithischia

The Ornithischian of the outgroup archosaurs originally called Thecodontia. They are predentary quadrotugal with long axis vertical, with palpebral bones. They have ossified tendons with the vertebral column. It has been suggested that Ornithischia are monophyletic.

Ornithischian dinosaurs which are not bird related, though the name 'Ornithischia' means bird-hipped. (Saurischia means lizard-hipped) were supposedly an evolution from theropod saurischian dinosaurs Ref Encyclopedia Britannica. All of them Herbivores. Their branch classification taxon is close to the Triceratops Horridus. Hadrosaurus seems to be the most popular of the Ornithischia.

The Ornithischian dinosaurs were mainly from the cretaceous period.

Nopesa in 1915 had suggested a subdivision within the Ornithischia. He proposed that between the bipedal and the ornithopods unarmoured, there should be an order Thyreophora. This included the ankylosaurus stegosaurus and the ceratopsians. However Norman and Sereno in 1984 stated that the ceratopsians were not of the Thyreophora.

Romer in 1956 proposed that Ornithischia was in four sub-orders. That was the Ornithopoda, the Stegosauria, the Ankl;yosauria and Ceratopsian with all bi=pedal forms.

Thulborn in 1971 proposed that the majority of Ornithischia were Iguanagontids, Pachycephlasauus, and Ceratopsians from the late Triassic to Cretaceous period. And the 'hypsilophodon plexus. Which were small Ornithopods.

Maryanska and Osmolska in 1974 proposed that Pachycephlasauria was an order of Ornithischia. In 1985 they proposed that Ankylosaurus and Stegosaurus did not share a common ancestor. They stated that Pacchycephlasauria and Ceratopsian formed a clade that excluded Ornithopods.

Sereno in 1984 stated that Fabrousoridae was monophyletic and that it was the basal of Ornithischia.

Ornithopods

The Heterodontasaurs had three kinds of teeth.

Dryosaurus small dinosaurs

Thescelosaurus

Camptosaurus, beaked dinosaurs

Iguanodontids dinosaurs with large claws

Ornithischia is in three suborders;

1,./ the first being were the bird footed, probably standing on all fours.

2./ Stegosauria armoured and quadrupedal

E.g. Stegosaurus with a cranial capacity of 56cc, spines 25in in length, believed to be of serial branch.

3./Ceratopsia, the horned dinosaurs E.g. the Triceratops, being of 20 to 25ft long.

Protoceratops was a Ceratopsian hornless and believed to be the descendent ancestral to Triceratops. (Ref John Klotz, Genes, Genesis and Evolution, pages 475)

No dinosaur fossils are found in the Tertiary rock. It is assumed that Pterosaurs were from the Jurassic and Cretaceous period. Ichthyosaurus was from the Mesozoic rock.

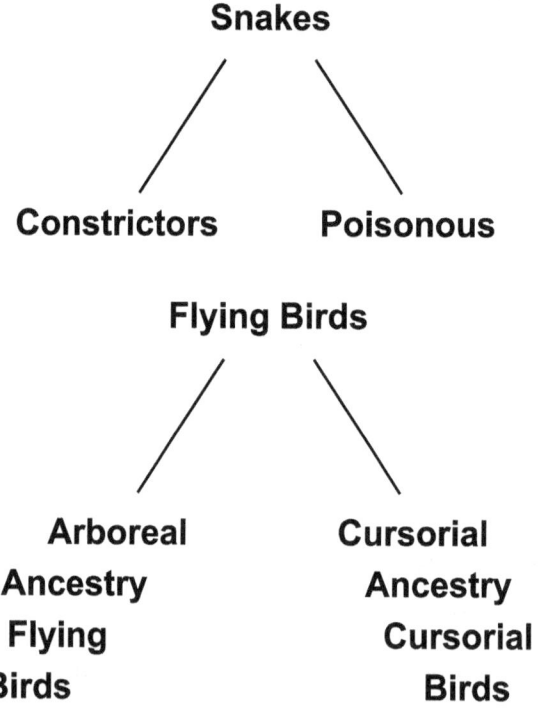

```
              Snakes
             /      \
            /        \
     Constrictors   Poisonous

           Flying Birds
           /         \
          /           \
     Arboreal        Cursorial
     Ancestry        Ancestry
     Flying          Cursorial
     Birds           Birds
```

The headless being the Archeopteryx. The other is the Archaeonis. These were both from the slate quarry at Solnhofen. These were both contemporaries of Compsognathus.

A contemporary of Archaeopteryx was the Archaeornis which was primitive to the Archaeornis a primitive Pterosaur Rhomphrycus.

All of the Ornithischia were herbivorous. They developed bizarre armour rather than bulk. The first of them are found from fossil tracks of the late Triassic rock. They are divided into three suborders where the Ornithopoda is first. The second order of the Ornithischia were the Stegosaurus, they were well armoured and quadrupedal.

Archeopteryx

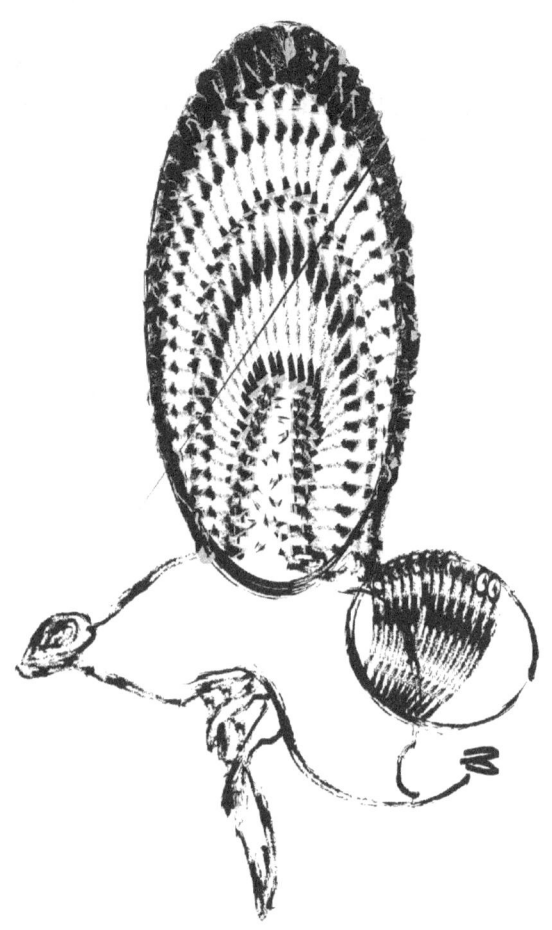

The best known of this suborder was the Stegosaurus, one of the most grotesque of all the dinosaurs. It had upstanding plates. The total weight of the animal was probably greater than any living elephant.

The next suborder of Ornithischia was the Ceratopsia or horned dinosaur. Mainly from North America, and some in Mongolia, the best known was the Triceratops which looked like a rhino of about 20 to 25ft in length.

The Mongolian Protoceratops was a ceratopsian, it was hornless and believed to have been an ancestor to the Triceratops. (Ref Edwin H. Colbert, The Dinosaur Book, 1951, pages 80-82)

(Ref John Klotz, Genes, Genesis and Evolution pages 473 to 475)

Extinction of Dinosaurs

Extinction of Dinosaurs puzzles paleontologists and evolutionists. No dinosaur fossils are found in Tertiary rock.

It has been suggested that they killed themselves off by intercine warfare. There were no signs of degeneration as they were still in their prime in Cretaceous times. Another aspect is that bloodthirsty mammals consumed dinosaur eggs, however, in Jurassic times these mammals were no bigger than kittens and there is no indication they were bloodthirsty.

Another theory was that there was a change in climate to the mountain building which followed the Cretaceous period.

Pakicetus

The Pakicetus looking like a small wolf-like animal was meant to be the transition from the living land animal to the whale, this is due to evolutionary theory. Pakicetus is the greek word for 'Pakistan Whale', where skeletons were found in the Punjab region. It's suborder was the Archeoceti. It was from the Eocene period 50million years ago. It was not found by the Tethys sea, but from adjacent river and floodplain deposits. It has a close relationship with hippos. Estimated length of Pakicetus 1 to 2 metres. It supposedly was at the early stage of evolution of the cetaceans.

Could Pakicetus have evolved into Maiacetus then to Orcinus. The reptile evolution suggests this. Its fossils however resembled that of creodonts.

There is also a theory that this animal also came from Peru, as a whale skeleton found there gave some clues. The bones were found in a 42.6 million year deposits off the coast of Peru, the finds were made by Mario Urbina, an author Musee de Historia Natural, in 2011, where the field expedition team gave the name 'Peregocetus Pacificus' meaning 'The traveling whale that reached the Pacific'

Olivier Lambert of the Royal Belgian Institute of Natural Sciences said;

'This is the first indisputable record of a quadruple whale skeleton of the whole Pacific Ocean, probably the oldest for the Americas, and the most complete outside India and Pakistan'

It has been said that Pakicetus was a transitional form between the Mesonychids and the Cetaceans.

In diagrams a typical transitional sequence of this 'whale evolution' from Pakicetus would be to Amblocetus, then to Basilosaurus then to Whales.

For this to be proven, let alone observed would take a vast amount of time. There is then transitional fossils if they could be found. The sequence, similarity would have to be so many.

Ambulocetus

Amblocetus was the walking whale. Supposedly from the Early Eocene period. It's size was similar to an alligator, around 11ft long 500 pounds. It was a Cetacean from Pakistan. It could move in salt and in freshwaters. It had invisible ears.

A specimen was found in the Upper Kuldana Formation of Eastern Pakistan, on a coastal area. An expedition team led by Johannes Thewissen of the Northeastern Ohio University College of Medicine, who found remains of a whale-like animal. They found it had a nose that allowed it to swallow underwater, and a periotic bone that enabled it to have enhanced hearing underwater. Its teeth were also similar to a whale.

It has been suggested by many paleontologists that Cetaceans are closely related to an extinct group of hoofed carnivorous animals called the mesonychians. Although there are similarities of the DNA and the proteins of Cetaceans, that microbiologists have noted the even-toed ungulates and the artiodactyls the hippopotamidae.

Ambulocetus 'The Walking Whale That Swam'. Lived in the Tethys Sea 49 million years ago. It lived 3 million years after Pakicetus and 9 million years after Basilosaurus.

Pterosaurs

The dinosaurs were one but one of the Mesozoic reptile groups. The group of flying lizards known as Pterosaurs. They flourished in the Jurassic and Cretaceous periods.

The Pterosaurs came in two groups: the Rhamphornchyoids and the Pterodactyloids; these were the descendants of the Pterosauria. The Ramphorcyhnus appeared first in the late

Triassic period then died out and became extinct in the late Jurassic. The Quezalcoatlus was one of the largest of the Pterosauria with an incredible wing span of 50ft or so.

Then there is the Pteranodon which was a more common of the Pterosauria. Its wingspan around 25ft with a light body of around 25 pounds with fragile bones was exceptionally good for gliding. It had stronger bones for the wings to enable maneuvers efficiently in flight.

The Pterosaurs were in two groups. The main two types were the Rhamphorhynchus and the Pterodactyl. Though there were other species Quetzacoatlus, worshipped by the Aztec God the Brasiel Dactylus from Brazil.

Ichthyosaurus

The ichthyosaurus constituted another of the Mesozoic reptile groups. These and the plesiosaurus dominated the seas from the Triassic and Upper Cretaceous period. They are believed to have derived from land living four foot reptiles, ranging from three to thirty feet. The eggs were believed to be hatched within the mother's body, so that the young were born alive.

The Ichthyosaurus had a shape and features of porpoises, and prehistoric dolphins. about 6 to 10ft in length, around 200 pounds This animal was a Piscivore. A specimen was discovered in the 1990's in Somerset.

It is regarded that Ichthyosaurs are a group within the Sauria and the Neodiapsida.

Eurhinosaurus was the Jurassic period of the Ichthyosaurus. The Stenopterygius was another species of Ichthyosaurus. Then the, Temnodontosaurus which was much larger at up to 30ft.

Turtles

Turtles were believed to have already existed in the Permian times. The tortoises and land-dwelling turtles have been known as fossils since the Eocene times. Modern sea turtles are supposed to have dated from the Cretaceous times. It is believed that there are marine turtles from the Upper Jurassic period. These are to have derived from a Permian lizard stock.

Snakes

Snakes makeup 2600 species today. Most of them are tropical. They are divided into two groups, constrictors and poisonous snakes.

Crocodiles and Alligators

The most ancient crocodiles came from the Triassic period and are more or less intermediate than crocodiles and dinosaurs.

Archeopteryx

John Ostrom an american palaeontology considered the arboreal theory as implausible, even Archaeopteryx;

'The critical point is that in order to fly, the animal first had to be able to climb. However, considering the design of modern birds, together with the oldest known bird, Archaeopteryx, that skill may have not been the repertoire of primitive birds, or even of bird ancestors.'

Birds from reptiles, how did the first mammals get breasts. How did a mammal get a four chamber-heart, instead of a three-chamber heart of the reptile. How was the reptile's blood temperature raised from 40c to nearly 100c in mammals? Evolutionists offer this gulf two fossils of what they call Archeopteryx.

The Archaeopteryx is also known as 'Urvogel' which in German means Original bird, which was discovered in Germany in 1860. Though Archaios is the Greek word for 'Ancient' and Pteryx means 'feather'. Its size was that of a pigeon. It was meant to be the 'missing link' of dinosaurs to birds. It is similar to Compsognathus.

It was not an exceptional flier. It probably took off vertically and then glided. Has it been extinct in the last 150 million years ago. Specimens found in Solnhofen in Lithographic Limestone dating up to 150 million years ago, The Jurassic period in Germany.

Its habitation was in salty lagoons, of a low tropical sea. According to its flight Julia Clarke a paleontologist of the University of Texas said about Archaeopteryx that modern flying birds have breast bones with keels which anchor the bird's downward stroke. Archeopteryx has not been found with bony breastbones. It has been suggested that it was a common pterosaur.

There were various specimens found The London Specimen found in 1861 near Langenaltheim. The Berlin specimen was found in 1877. The Maxburg specimen found in 1958. The Teyler (Haarlem) specimen was found near Reidenburg in 1855. The Eichstatt Specimen was found in 1951 near Wokerszell.

(One metre of rock deposition is roughly equal to 5000 years of deposition.)

According to one nature report, Archeopteryx had a running speed of 2 metres per second. The minimum required running speed is 6 metres per second. The arboreal kind take off from trees. The cursorial kind takes off from running.

There are mathematical equations for a model of Archeopteryx, weighing 0.2kg flapping its wings at 9.3 Hz.

$$Vf = Fs \; \emptyset \; by$$

Fs is sum of strokes per second 18.6
$\emptyset$ is the angle subtended by the wings during the downstroke (50 degrees)
b is the wingspan (0.58m)
Vflap is the average flapping velocity

This theory/formula was given by Rayner and Yalden.

Reptile Characteristics

The Mesozoic era has been called the age of the reptiles, where they mainly dominated the earth. This being the period of dinosaurs. The development of the embryo produced an amnion. It is supposed to represent an ancestral aquatic environment. An allantois is also believed to have been present in the development of a dinosaur egg.

(Ref John Klotz, Genes Genesis and Evolution page 483)

Crocodiles and Alligators

Crocodiles and Alligators make up to Loricata or Crocodilia. The most ancient crocodiles came from the Triassic period. Which were more or less intermediate between the crocodiles and dinosaurs.

(Ref John Klotz, Genes Genesis and Evolution page 483)

Birds

J.H. Ostrom 'Bird Flight, How Did It Begin?' page 204, 46, 1979.

This is J. Ostrom's account on bird flight;

'Previous speculations on this question have produced two quite different scenarios. Stated very simply, these are that birds begin to fly 'from the trees down, or from the ground up.

1./Arboreal Theory, :From the trees down, which is logical and widely favoured.

2./Cursorial Theory: 'From the ground up, this theory is less probable.

It is believed that flying birds had an arboreal ancestry. The cursorial birds had terrestrial ancestry.

Those who believe that birds originated from arboreal, or tree-dwelling ancestors believe that in purely cursorial animals the grasping hind toe tends to vanish and the front limbs tend to reduce in size. The ancestors were believed to be divided into two groups, the first returned to the ground and became dinosaurs, and the other group became birds. (Ref John Klotz, Genes, Genesis and Evolution pages 484 to 485)

The earliest of birds are from two known specimens, one of these is the headless known as Archaeopteryx. The other is known as Archaeonis. They both came from the slate quarry at Solnhofen Bavaria. These were contemporaries of Compsognathus the smallest dinosaur, a contemporary of Archaeopteryx And Archaeornis was the primitive pterosaur Rhamphorhyncus.

In Cretaceous times there were two fossils, Hesperornis and Ichthyornis, Hesperornis was about 4.5 ft in length, with powerful hind limbs and was used in swimming, awkward on land. It had lost its ability to fly. It is believed to be similar to modern looms, but it was flightless.

The Ichthyornis was a small ternlike bird, a good flyer. Believed to be quite modern except for the fact it still had teeth. Tertiary birds had a loss of flight numerous times during the Tertiary period.

(Ref John Klotz, Genes Genesis and Evolution pages 484 to 487)

D. Savile on "Adaptive Evolution in the Avian wing" page 222, 1957, his comments on the structure of the Archaeopteryx wing;

'The eight primates are graduated proximally and distally to form a nearly elliptical wing tip of surprisingly modern appearance...... The wings were not preserved in fully extended position, but they seem to have been nearly elliptical in outline, and except for the lack of an alula or emarginate primaries, are not unlike those of many passerines in general appearance'.

The Seymouria an reptile-like amphibian is described as;

'A modest form from the Permian exhibits such a combination of amphibian and reptilian characters that it's proper position in the classification of the vertebrates has been much disputed..... Seymouria thus seems....almost exactly on the dividing line between amphibian and reptiles'.

It is evident that Archaeopteryx its brain was avian, avian cerebral hemispheres and cerebellum, Ref, Jerison "Brain Evolution and Archaeopteryx 1968.

In the Upper Oolithe, in the lithographic stone quarries of Solnhofen 1862, were the remains of bird Archaeopteryx, about the size of a rook. Professor Owen says it's not.

Chordates

Chordates are human and animal phylum and vertebrates which is a part of the Deuterostome Kingdom Chordates have a notochord and a dorsal neural tube. They have pharyngeal slits that connect the pharynx to the neck.The slits filter the food out of the water. Chordates have a post anal tail.

chordate s consist of three types;

1./ Cephalochordates, these are of 35 species, small fish-like creatures.

2./ Urochordates, these are of 3000 extant species, tadpoles plankton, ascidians.

3./Tunicates and Vertebrates these have an endoskeleton, neural crest which means the development of head and jaws from a lancelet-like ancestor. The endoskeleton has a vertebrate cartilage Neural Crest the embryonic cells develop into craniofacial cartilage and bone., smooth muscles and melanocytes.

The Hindus, Charaka made distinctions of the Jarayuja (invertebrates) and the Anadaja (vertebrates) in 500BC. Aristotle established the Enaima (vertebrates) and the Anima (invertebrates) in 300BC.

There are no chordates in Cambrian rock. Protochordates are found in Silurian rock. Primitive chordates gave rise to Amphioxus that develop into ascidians. Ascidians have a nerve cord that only has larvae and a notochord.

The second type of development is from Amphioxus, similar to Ostracoderms. This gave rise to modern fish. The basic ostracoderms gave rise to related cephalochordates, which gave rise to ascidians.

(Ref Genes Genesis and Evolution pages 457, 458, John Klotz 1955)

Ostracoderm means 'shellskin' It is believed that it gave rise to groups of lamprey eels and relatives to cyclostomes. These have a cartilaginous skeleton and are parasites.

Mammals

It is believed they branched off from a reptile stock at an early stage. It is believed they are descendents of the therapsid order of reptiles, which appeared in the Permian period. The therapsids were abundant in the Middle and Upper Permian of South Africa. These later gave rise to cynodonts, named for their dog-like teeth. They were divided into incisors, canines, and molars. They are believed to be similar to Tidosaurus, another therapsid group of South Africa.

The therapsid reptiles were "single arched". The birds were derived from the "two-arched" archosaurian reptiles. "The one-arched" and "Two-arched" conditions refer to the one and two temporal arches of each side of the skull. The archosaurs gave rise to the crocodiles, dinosaurs, Sphendon, lizards and snakes.

The mammals are the only descendants of the therapsid or "one-arched" reptiles.

The two class characteristics of the mammals are the possession of hair and mammary glands. Both are difficult to account for evolution. It has been suggested that hair is the counterpart of feathers in birds, and that has developed from reptiles. As hair develops from connective tissue, hair develops from epithelial tissue. Feathers have a blood supply which hair lacks. The two are not homologous.

The archosauria gave rise to the Crocodiles Dinosaurs, Sphenoid lizards, snakes.

The first mammals were found in the Upper Triassic strata, Germany, England, South Africa, China.

The oldest known mammals were the Tritylodon.

Early Mammal Evolution

The first mammals are found in the upper Triassic strata in Germany, England and South Africa and China. They were then found later in the Jurassic of eastern Wyoming, and in the late Cretaceous in that same region.

The oldest known mammal is the Tritylodon found in the Upper Triassic in South Africa and China. The Pantotheria was another mammal found in the various Jurassic strata.

Archaic Mammals

These mammals are believed to begin their evolution in the early Tertiary times. They became deficient to get food and thus became extinct. Archaic mammals included marsupials and five groups of placental mammals.

One of the Tertiary placental mammals was the flesh-eating carnivorous Creodonta. Doglike bearlike, hyenalike.

The Condylartha were a group of primitive ungulates with heavy tails, short legs.

The Amblypoda, heavy, large, lived in swamps.

The Monotremes lay eggs before hatching and live on the yolk contained in the egg. Monotremes are found in New Guinea and Tasmania. They include the platypus, duckbill, the Echidna. The characteristics are believed to be developed from birds and monotremes by convergent evolution.

Gregory believes that the monotremes originated from an early marsupial stock rather than Triassic pro-mammals. There is no fossil record of the monotremes, only extinct Echidna-like fossils, this dates from the Pleistocene period found in Australia. (Ref John Klotz, Genes, Genesis and Evolution pages 489 -493)

Marsupials

The marsupials are believed to have originated from the close of the Cretaceous period.,and before placental mammals. They are divided into three suborders, the Ployprodontia, Diprotodontia, Caenolestidae.

Polyprodontia- Insectivorous, carnivorous

Diprotodontia -herbivorous

Caenolestidae, shrews from South America.

There is still uncertainty whether Monotremes, Marsupials, placentals as to which came first. The placenta in the Australian skinks is believed to be an example of convergent evolution.

99% of the biology of any organism resides in it's soft anatomy, which is inaccessible in a fossil. (Ref Micheal Denton, Evolution, A Theory In Crisis, page 177, 1996)

Chapter 2

Entropy

The rule that entropy increases came to be as known as the law of entropy or the second law of thermodynamics.

(Ref Robert E.D. Clark, The Universe Plan or Accident, page 20, 1961)

Boltzmann was able to calculate entropy accurately from a knowledge of the number and positions of atoms.

Newton claimed that the entropy law was an argument for believing that in a distant past God had created the world.

(Ref Robert E.D. Clark, The Universe Plan or Accident, page 20, 25, 1961)

Joseph McCabe wrote "The Riddle of The Universe Today, page 29, 1934"

"To deny that there is, in the obscure depths of space, a compensating or restoring mechanism is an unscientific and illogical piece of dogmatism. There is no use appealing to thermodynamic wars".

J. Needham "History is on Our Side" page 212, 1946 said;

"The ever-present possibility of cyclical trends.... Or a continuous flow of energy through the universe, make deductions from the entropy law unconvincing"

(Ref Robert E.D. Clark, The Universe Plan or Accident, page 29, 1961)

The Author Robert E.D. Clark gave this example of entropy using cubes, size, proportion, volume and how it could apply to the entropy law, here is what he said;

"Imagine a space to be divided up into a number of zones - say, cubical in the Shape and the side of r. Then all the radiation gravitational force etc,. Which passes from one zone to another must pass through the surface of the cube, and it's quantity will be proportional to its surface, and so to r2. But the total mass of matter inside the cube will be proportional to its volume, that is to r3.. Imagine larger and larger cubes, the interaction between them will get less and less and less when considered in relation to the quantity of matter that they contain. That is to say, the larger they become, the more nearly they will approach isolation from the rest of the universe. In an infinite universe, we may consider indefinitely large cubes and make them as isolated as we please. But since it is agreed that the entropy law would apply to each one of these isolated cubes separately, it must also apply to each one of an infinite number of them - that is, it applies to the whole universe"

Universe, Plan or Accident, page 30, 1961.

Entropy can be considered from two standpoints, a thermodynamic variable of the system under consideration. (Ref Walter E. Lammerts page 67), and measure of elementary particles atoms, molecules that can be arranged from a solid state. The concept of entropy is the conditions where heat can be converted into work. The quantity of heat 1 (2 dQ necessary to bring a system from state 1 to state 2 is not uniquely defined since it depends on the path followed from 1 to 2.. Thermodynamic quantity 1) 2 dQ /T, where T is the absolute temperature, and has a value which is independent of the path followed. This is true if the path is reversible, and the integration is carried out so that each quantity of the heart is divided by the temperature at which it is introduced. This quantity is calculated from a temperature of absolute zero is called the entropy (S)

$$S = 0\frac{dQrev}{T}$$

Some systems have solid solutions that have a finite value of entropy, even at absolute zero. The measurement of the entropy depends on the quantity of heat. Entropy in an isolated system tends to a maximum.

Classical thermodynamics is concerned with the macroscopic systems. If the energy content of a particular system is known, then each of the molecules will not necessarily have the same energy. If the system is raised from T 1 to T 2, thermodynamically it is considered a single event. The atomic level an immense number of collisions of molecules occurs. A thermodynamic state consists of many states on the atomic scale. The possibilities of realization are called micro-states. This can be defined as entropy, S = k ln w, k is Boltzmann's constant,

$$\frac{K = R}{N}$$

R is the constant per mole. N is Avogadro's number. Entropy tends to a maximum, according to the equation it's a tendency to a most probable state. Second law does not hold entirely rigidly. The question then is what is the most probable state? The state which has the most number of microstates. Entropy is classed as micro-states vs measuring quantities of heat.

Duane Gish

Evolutionary theory contradicts the Second Law of Thermodynamics. Sir Julian Huxley defined the second law as;

'There is a general tendency of all observed systems to go from order to disorder, reflecting dissipation of energy available for future transformations-the law of increasing entropy.

Entropy also measures randomness, or lack of orderliness of the system; the greater the randomness, the greater the entropy.

I.Asimov 'Smithsonian Institute page 6 June 1970, quoted;

'The universe is constantly getting more disorderly!, viewed that way, we can see the Second Law all about us............In fact all we have to do is nothing, and everything deteriorates, collapses, breaks down, wears out, all by itself, and that is what the second law is all about'

Comparison of the Second Law of Thermodynamics, as defined by J. Huxley:

'Evolution in the extended sense can be defined as a directional and essentially irreversible process occurring in time, which in its course gives rise to an increase in variety and an increasingly high level of organization in it's products. Our present knowledge indeed forces us to the view that the whole of reality is evolution - a single process of self-transformation.' (Ref Oliver Barclay, Creation and Evolution page 145, 1985).

According to this, there is a tendency for natural systems to go from disorder to order. It is believed that particles evolved into people. There must be a contradiction in Huxley's process.

The Second Law of Thermodynamics applies only to closed systems. If the system is open to an external source of energy, it is asserted, complexity can be generated and maintained within the expense of the energy supplied to it from the outside. Since our solar system is an open system, and the energy is supplied from sun to the earth, decrease in entropy, or increase in order, on the earth during the evolutionary process has been more than compensated by an increase in entropy, decrease in order on the sun. End result a net decrease in order.

The Second Law of Thermodynamics has not been violated. (Ref Oliver Barclay, Creation and Evolution, page 146, 1985)

Entropy Principle as a Universal Law

Dr. H. M. Morris, suggested that the principle energy increase is a direct result of the curse God placed on the creation as a result of Adam's sin. (Gen 3: 17-19)

The first law states although energy can be converted from one form to another, the total amount remains unchanged. Energy is neither created or being destroyed at the present time.

The second law states that although the total amount of energy in any closed mechanical system remains unchanged, there is always a tendency for it to become less available for future work.

If energy cannot be added or subtracted, it must originally have been created. This requires an external cause - a creator. The entropy law contradicts the central evolutionary affirmation that life forms can evolve upwards towards increasing complexity.

Some evolutionists have sought to refute the obvious challenge of the law of entropy by contending that it applies to closed systems, whereas the earth is an open system, since it interacts with the sun, moon, other bodies in space receiving and emitting matter.

There is no evidence of a source within this large closed system which could or did provide the information needed to effect the upward evolution of life forms. (Ref Colin Mitchell, Case for Creation pages 48 -49, 1994)

Marx, who wrote the book 'Das Kapital' which had strong views against capitalism, dedicated this book to Darwin, Darwin received the letter from Marx in 1880 regarding this. Darwin showed no interest in Marx's economics or politics.(Ref Donald Patten, Biblical Flood and The Ice Epoch pages 12,13).

During the 19th Century, as uniformitarianism expanded rapidly (in biology and geology) were greatly enthused. Catastrophists were confused and dismayed. Geological Catastrophism became a "dying" species. It was unscientific. Uniformitarianism caused in many cultures, upheavals.

Chapter 3

The Flood

There have been theories that the flood was caused by prolonged cyclonic storms, but rain could not cause a global flood, these would be classed as uniformitarianism. The flood being local would hold uniformitarianism as being true. The catastrophic view would mean an extra-terrestrial gravitational field on the earth, then the global flood is plausible.

If the flood were local, the flood may have come from one or two regions of the earth, but the flood has accounted for nearly 40 different areas of the hemisphere. Hebrew tradition says that Shem was a survivor of the flood was the oldest man on earth in the patriarchal age, quote from Henry H. Halley's Bible handbook 1959, if Halley's theory is right then Melchizedek is either Shem, Arphaxad, Salah or Eber.

The Hebrews account is that the ark was grounded in the high Ararat-Caucasus-Elburz region. These areas have heights of around 17,000 feet, and 8000 and 10,000 feet above mean sea level. The topography of these areas may give hints to the tides of the flood. There are three lakes of the Armenia region which can be considered at the minimum level at which the ark was grounded. Lake Urmia in Iran is 4,364 ft above sea level. Lake Van in Turkey is 5,620ft, then its Lake Sevan in Russia 6,345 ft. The exact resting place of the ark has not been confirmed. But it's fair to assume it had rested in the vicinity of this area being 8000 feet above sea level. However, the altitude and topography of the

Ararat area would meet the conditions for the resting place of the Ark, for tides 10,000 feet and greater, below and above the antediluvian sea level.

If the flood had been caused by atmospheric precipitation, the ark would have floated downwards, and in response solely to the gravity of the earth. (Ref Donald Patten The Biblical Flood, ice Age Epoch page 59, 1970)

If the estimate of compression is 2 tons per sq inch, 300 tons per/sq ft., water 62lbs per cubic ft.

10,000 cubic ft water in vertical position is 629,000 lbs of pressure, and is just over 2 tons per sq inch.

(Ref Donald Patten The Biblical Flood, ice Age Epoch page 62, 1970)

With reference to Genesis 7, it says the waters increased and prevailed on the earth, the waters flooded mountains, valleys, plateaus etc., a 'second gravity' which opposes the gravity of the earth has been suggested that caused these tidal upheavals.

Evolution and uniformitarianism practically required agnosticism, and they made atheism increasingly respectable, even virile. Modern uniformitarianism was conceived over 200 years ago. !00 years ago it was the dominant theory of the history of the earth. It advocates maintained that our planet and our solar system have had a serene past in terms of multiplied millions of years.(Ref. Donald Patten, The Biblical Flood and the Ice Epoch 1966 page 2) Uniformitarianism; the doctrine that existing processes acting as present, are sufficient to account for all geological changes.

Flavius Josephus gave an account of the nature of the flood;

"When God gave the signal, it began to rain, the water poured down for forty days, till it became 15 cubits higher than the earth's surface, which was the reason why there were no greater number preserved, since they had no place to flee to. When the rain ceased, the water began to abate"

The uniformitarian principle would be correct of a localized flood. The catastrophic view would be correct if an extraterrestrial gravitational field had affected the earth for a global flood. If the flood had been of local phenomena, it must have been based on climatological principles, like rain. If it were a global phenomena then immense magnitude, oceans would be involved.

Water-lain strata if it is on a global scale, below and above the mean sea level, remains unexplained for a local flood concept. It would be considered that floods would have occurred in one or two regions of the earth. The bible teaches that rain was associated with the flood, but it was not the primary cause.

(Ref Donald Patten The Biblical Flood, ice Age Epoch page 62, 1970)

If the rain in the atmosphere could hold and then were to condense immediately the volume of precipitation would be less than 12 inches in any one location. If the atmosphere were composed of pure water vapour and then suddenly condensed, it would amount to 30ft of water, not enough for the flood.

(Ref Donald Patten The Biblical Flood, ice Age Epoch page 63, 1970)

The water vapour canopy works by

1./ It prevents the sun's short wave radiation reaching the ground level. This is buttressed and the effect of the ozone of the canopy. The human eye cannot see this. (Eyes can see wavelengths of 3000 to 8000 Angstrom units.

The length of Noah's months is not absolutely certain. The account says that the flood started on 17/2/600 and that the waters prevailed for 150 days, during the latter part of which they were 'returning from off the earth' After the ark rested on 17/7/600. If all Noah's months had 30 days and we include the day on which the flood started and also the sixteenth of Nisan, but not the actual day on which the ark rested, we shall have 14+30+30+30+30+16 = 150. And this seems the most likely as the word 'after' seems to exclude the seventeenth Nisan itself from the 150. If, on the other hand, Noah included, as later Hebrew chronologists did, both the initial and final days we can only obtain 150 by making one of the months 29 days, thus 14+30+30+30+30+16 = 150

(Ref The Flood Reconsidered Fredk A. Filby, page 106, 1970)

The waters according to Genesis 8.5 went down slowly for another two and a half months until on the first day of the 10th month (About 14th June). The tops of the surrounding heights could be seen. Noah waited 40 days more - bringing him to about the tenth day of the eleventh month (July 24)

(Ref The Flood Reconsidered Fredk A. Filby, page 109, 1970)

The Hebrew account specifies the mountains (plural) of Ararat suggesting that the name is used for a district and not for a particular peak 2 Kings 19.37 Isaiah 37.38 Jeremiah 51.27.

(Ref The Flood Reconsidered Fredk A. Filby, page 114, 1970)

If there had been no flood in Noah's day, based upon the race's rate of doubling, i.e., once in 146.13 years, since Noah begat Shem, there would be since the 6060 years from Adam and Eve's creation 41.35 doublings; and raised 2 to its power is 2,583,852,323,274, which would be the earth's present population had there been no flood in Noah's day. This is about 2,500 times its present population.

In Palestine, one of Abraham's early experiences was his meeting with Melchisadek, to whom he tithed, and from whom he received communion emblems, Priest-King of Salem, (Jerusalem). Hebrew tradition says:

He was Shem, survivor of the flood, who was still alive, earth's oldest living man, priest in the patriarchal age, of the whole race. If so, it is a hint, that, this early right after the flood, God chose Jerusalem to be the scene of human redemption.``

Morris and Whitcomb, The Genesis Flood page 121, Their statement on the flood was that the oceans mass is estimated at 1.37×10 power 18 metric tonnes, and the atmospheric water as 1.3×10 power 13. Thus the total rainfall could only add one part in the 100,000 to the volume of the oceans, increasing the mean depth by 0.12 ft , about 4 inches.

The earth is an oblate spheroid it rotates with a circumferential speed of over 1000 miles per hour at the equator, and with intermediate speeds in intermediate latitudes. One result of this is that the Earth's equatorial crust has bulged, due to the centrifugal motion of the magma. The equatorial diameter is 27 miles greater than is the polar diameter. If there were a relocation of the poles, there would necessarily be a relocation of the equator, and with the earth in rotational motion, there would be a relocation of the equatorial bulge zone. This requires an expansion of the earth's crust, a cleavage or a tearing perpendicular to the equator and wider in the equatorial zones than in the sub-tropical extremities.

(Ref Donald Patten The Biblical Flood, ice Age Epoch page 253, 1970)

And from the above criteria, the Rift Valley of Africa meets this requirements;

1./It is perpendicular to the equator.

2./Widest in the equatorial zone.

3./Most complex in the equatorial zone..

This orogenital cleavage coupled with another similar to the one in the mid-Atlantic range coupled with the two zones of orogenic uplift linked with a astral catastrophic thought, is suggestive that there was a major relocation of the earth's axis, and the two geographical poles, during the flood catastrophe.

This scientist had this to say;

"After all, it is easy to convince oneself that it is neither in one and same time, nor by the effect of the deluge, that the sea left uncovered the continents which we inhabit; because it is certain, by the testimony of sacred books, that the earthly paradise was in Asia, and Asia was a continent inhabited before the deluge; in consequence, it is not in that time that the seas covered considerable parts of the globe. So the earth was, before the deluge, broadly the same as she today; and that enormous quantity of water, which the divine justice brought down on the earth to punish the culpable men, caused infant death to all creatures; but it had produced not a single alteration on the earth's surface; it destroyed not even the plants, because the pigeon brought back an olive-branch"

Location of the Ark, its Elevation

A record of the Hebrews, corroborated by the Middle-Eastern traditions, is that the Ark was grounded high in the Ararat-Caucasus-Elburz region. The elevations in this complex rise to 17000 ft above the mean sea level. The elevations being 8000 to 10000 ft above the mean sea, indicate the topography may be a clue to the magnitude of the flood tides in the area.(Ref Donald Patten Biblical Flood Ice Epoch page 54)

If we examine the region of Armenia, three nations Iran, Russia, Turkey the area where the ark rested, and the topography of its lakes i.s. Lake Urmia largest 4,364ft above mean sea level, in Iran, Lake Van, Turkey 5,260ft., Lake Gokcha, Russia 6,345ft above mean sea-level, so it is fair to believe that the ark was 8 to 10000ft above the mean sea-level. The altitude and topography of the Ararat region is indicative of the election of the final resting place of the Ark. This is the basis assuming tides of at least 10,000ft, above and below the mean antediluvian sea-level. (Ref Donald Patten, Biblical Flood Ice Epoch page 59)

Consider, therefore, the broadness of the flood. The Eurasian landmass is the largest one on the face of our planet. It comprises about 57% of the land area in the world, including it's African appendage. The Ark was grounded at the heart of the region; about 2000 miles from the Arabian Sea.

The ark has landed in the interior region of the land of Eurasia, it comprises 57% of the land area of the world. The ark is grounded about 2000 miles from the Arabian sea, 2500 miles from the Barents sea, 3000 miles from the atlantic ocean, 5000 miles from the pacific ocean.

Tides occur twice every 24half hours on the earth's surface. If there were tidal conditions, with water 5,000 to 10,000 ft above the mean sea-level, pressure on the earth's crust would have mounted to 300 tons per square ft. (2 tons per square inch). This can compress any sediment, metamorphose deposits into successive strata. As layer upon layer of sedimentary rock has been laid down by immense pressure. This makes a strong case for oceanic tides above the mean sea level.

Oceanic seas cover the bulk of the earth's surface 72%. If the atmosphere could hold, the volume of precipitation would be less than 12 inches in any one location. If the atmosphere were composed of pure water vapour, then suddenly condensed it would amount to 30ft water. The oceans of the earth there are more than 200,000,000 cubic miles of water, it is enough to drown ¾ of the present surface of the earth, some of it from depths 10,000 to 30,000ft. (Ref Donald Patten Biblical Flood Ice Epoch pages 62 to 64)

Genesis 6 and 7, has sometimes been meant the entire globe, as explained by Marcel de Serres in a learned book "La Cosmogonie de Moise " as being an accurate translation. He has proved that the hebrew word (haaretz) translated "the earth"is often used in the sense of region or country.

If all the water existing in the oceans, seas, rivers, and atmosphere, was deposited upon the globe, and equally divided over its surface, such as the universal sea would only be about 2 ½ miles in depth. 30 times as much would have been required to form a casing of water that would have covered all the mountains of the world. Another miracle would have been necessary to get rid of this enormous extra quantity of water of 1000 millions of cubic miles.

Moses said that the waters prevailed 15 cubits upwards, he implied that he did not know the exact amount of waters, only that it had risen more than 26 ft. If 29,000ft had been intended, that would have been necessary to cover Mount Everest.

(Ref Samuel Kinns PH. D.,F.R.A.S The Harmony of the Bible With Science page 398, 1895)

The ark was to be 300 cubits long by 50 cubits wide, and 30 cubits high. If we assume the cubit to be about 18 inches, the overall dimensions would be 450ft x 75ft x 45ft. Giving a total volume, if taken as a rectangular box of 1,518,750 cubic feet. This on the modern reckoning of gross tonnage for modern ships, would be equivalent to a vessel of 15,000 tons, this is not the actual weight of the vessel. Taking the ark as being made of cypress wood with the planks one foot thick, allowing two extra decks or floors, and reasonable longitudinal and cross walls, we can calculate that it would require something like 280,000 cubic feet of timber, which at about 530oz per cubic ft gives a dead weight of about 4140 tons. Again, if we take the ocean water as 35 cubic feet per ton such a vessel completely empty would float with about 4.3 feet below water. To load it to a depth of 15 feet would require 10,000 tons of cargo and to 20 feet, 15,000 tons.

If we assume, the weight of the animals as 100 tons, and if we allow each animal 20 times its own weight of food and 20 times its weight of water for a year we should have a cargo of 4100 tons.

(Ref The Flood Reconsidered Fredk A. Filby page 88 1970)

The Bible states that the ark landed on the mountains (plural) of Ararat, indicating that it was in a district not a peak. Josephus said the Armenians called the Ark's landing place Apobaterion -'Place of Descent, Disembarking' Nicolaus of Damascus called it the mountains Baris.

Noah's Ark barge like vessel, which floated not sailed

It has been called 'Lubar' by Epiphanius which means 'descending place' . William de Rubruquis in about AD 1253 said that in Armenia there was a town called Nachuan, Armenia, called Masis, and another place called 'Cemainum' it means 'eight' memory of the eight people saved by the ark.

Ancient historian Moses Chorenensis quoted a place called 'Naschidsheuan' - 'place of descent'. There is a town in Armenia called 'Nakhichevan' meaning the possible burial place of Noah, 160 km south-east of Ararat.

The Greenhouse Effect

Plant life was more luxuriant in the earlier age was that it had to do with the proportions of carbon dioxide and water vapour in the atmosphere, the principle of long-wave radiation of the heat from earth, and a greenhouse effect. The Earth receives short-wave, medium and long-wave radiation from the sun during the day. It converts this into long-wave radiation which it re-radiates in space, during both the day and the nighttime.

If there had been a canopy of water vapour enshrouding the earth, during the antediluvian period,this would have greatly reduced the temperature differentials at the Earth's surface.

Earth has three types of winds, the planetary wind system, the seasonal monsoon, the diurnal land, sea breeze, similar to the monsoon.

There are three types of rain, convective, cyclonic and orographic. The Biblical record indicates that the Earth in an antediluvian era was a luxuriant place for flora, vegetation. The Bible says there was no rain, the Earth was watered by mist or dew at night, Genesis 2:6. If there were a canopy of water vapour, it would have been an abundant atmospheric constituent. (Ref Donald Patten

Biblical Flood, Ice Epoch page 202). It is proposed that the antediluvian canopy condensed with the intrusion of particles of astral ice, which was one phase of the flood. (Ref Donald Patten Biblical Flood, Ice Epoch page 204)

Catastrophists consider the Alps to have been raised up suddenly. This being a global uplift, with both tidal sides of the magma and the lesser but yet very considerable inundation of watery tides. Uniformitarianism considers that one portion of the Alps was raised about 185,000,000BC and 27,000,000 years later, a second portion was raised, and then 31,000,000 years later around 125,000,000BC The Alps dated between 125,000,000BC and 185,000,000BC The dating of this uplift with the flood would be 2800BC +,- 500 years. This would be approximately 5000 years ago. This is a differential of about 99.997%. Lyell's placing of the Ice epoch at 1,000,000 years ago is a difference of 99,8% (Ref Donald Patten The Biblical Flood Ice Epoch, page 95)

Uniformitarianism considered that the ark to have rested on Mount Ararat was impossible, as rain could not have caused this, but the tidal movement could have done this. The Ark was stranded on the second highest mountains in the eastern hemisphere, this area termed by political geographers, such as Mackinder, as the 'heartland' region. If the following is taken into account, the Eurasian mass is the largest of the planet 57% of the land area of the planet. The ark is grounded 2,000 miles from the Arabian sea (Indian Ocean). 2,500 miles from the Barents sea, 3,000 miles from the Atlantic Ocean, 5,000 miles from the Pacific Ocean. As the Ark rested in this heartland, the flood had to be tidal. If there was atmospheric precipitation the ark would have floated downward. Any rainfall would have been concentrated in maritime areas. Noah's boat was a barge, not a ship, it was built for floating not for sailing.

Events of the Flood

When taking into account Genesis 7:17, the waters increased and bored up the ark and rose above the earth, then in Genesis 7:24, the waters increased for 150 days, 'the waters increased, the waters rose higher, waters steadily receded' these fit descriptions of tidal waves. Tides occur around twice in every 24 half hours, where the tides increase continually. In Genesis 7 and 8 the length of time of the flood totalled 371 days. Genesis 7;12, 7:24, 8:5, 8:6-7, 8:8, 8:10 (Another 7 days lapsed), 8:12, 8:13, 8:14.

The tidal waves, severe pressure is a result of the Earth's sedimentary layers twice daily. Tidal conditions with water 5000 to 10000 feet above sea level, the pressure on the earth would be around 300 tons per square foot, 2 tons per square inch. This enormous pressure could metamorphose deposits into strata. With fauna, flora turning into debris, then into fossils.

Layers of sedimentary rock, layer after layer, by great pressures makes the global catastrophes possible, oceanic tides of great elevations above sea level. The Foundations of the deep of the antediluvian oceans could mean the following that the earth 72% covered by seas, oceans, that rain and oceanic tides caused the flood by deranged sweeping of them both together in large volumes. If rain were to condense in the atmosphere the volume of precipitation would be less than 12inches at any one location. If the atmosphere had pure water which then condensed it would give around 30ft of water, which would not be enough for a global flood and to hold a barge. If the earth had 200,000,000 cubic miles of water, it would drown ¾ of the earth's surface. It is known that depths of even 10,000 have drowned some areas. Rain is the rising action, it contributed .04 to 1 half % of the water. The foundations of the deep contributed 99.96%.

Period When Deluge Waters Fell

With reference to this period, Whitcomb and Morris commented "The newly deposited sediments were still relatively soft and unconsolidated. The imposition of new gradients and currents over them when the land began to rise would have immediately induced a scouring system on a large scale. The mixture of water and mud thus formed would, in flowing downslope, itself cause tremendous submarine erosion and ultimate deposition". Turbidity currents must have been many.

Lack of space, prevents the continued enunciation of the arguments for cataclysmal deposition, the following might be at the front 1./ the thanatocoenosis or "fossil graveyards" 2./ The preservation of soft parts, 3./The stratification as an indication of some recurrent tidal wag ve. (Ref Walter E. Lammerts Why Not Creation page 164).

In the Netherlands, the Mesozoic is covered everywhere. Triassic limestones are covered only with thin beds of Pleistocene till or niveo-aeolian cover sands.

In Huttonian geology, it was assumed that the limestone sequences were deposited by the settling of calcareous skeletons of the marine micro- and macro-organisms. Van Straaten supposed that the north half of the Adriatic some 20 grams of lime per square meter per annum. 0.00008cm per annum is deposited.

Regards to Winterswijk Limestone, for sedimentary environments, no ephemeral markings could have been rapidly covered. For the ephemeral markings, in their good condition, is that the lime beds must have been rapidly deposited after each other. It means that, Calcareous materials were not auto, but allochthonous.

Flood Traditions

Stickling reported that anthropologists have collected 59 Flood legends from three aborigines of North America. 46 from Central and South America. 31 from Europe, 23 from Asia. 17 from the Middle East, (Ref J.A. Stickling, A Statistical analysis of flood legends 1972, pages 152-155)

The names are given to men for flood events, Noh in Sudan, Nu-u in Hawaii, Nu-Wah in China.

Chinese tradition assigns the flood to 2300BC. The symbol for 'ship' in Chinese is made up of a boat of eight mouths. This shows the ship carried eight people.

The Indian Vedas have two flood accounts; Rig-Veda, Manu builds himself an ark. Another of a similar name builds one himself. (Ref Colin Mitchell, Case for Creationism, page 161, 1994)

Berossus, a Chaldean priest contemporary with Alexander the Great, reported the flood occurred in the reign of the 10th King of Babylon.

The god Chronos warned Xisuthros, king of Babylon, to build a ship to save his family, friends and animals . The size was five stadia long by 2 wide (approx 1,000 x 400 metres). Xisuthros sent out birds. The first two returned, but not the third. Xisuthros disembarked with his wife, daughter and pilot. He raised an altar, sacrificed to the gods, and then disappeared to heaven with them. The others disembarked from the ark. Xisuthros was not found, but a voice heard that he was in heaven with his family.

The voice then told them to return to Babylon, and to dig up the writings at Sippara and to make them known, and to tell them they had landed in Armenia. (Ref Colin Mitchell, Case for Creationism, page 161, 1994). They went to Babylon, dug up the writings, founded by temples, and restored Babylon.

The Greeks had a tradition, that Zeus destroyed the whole world, where Deucalion was saved. The Romans tradition was that Ovid's 'metamorphoses' Jupiter destroys the human race with a flood. A man called Deucalion and his wife Pyrrha were saved.

An epic of Flood stories is the Gilgamesh Epic. It is in cuneiform inscription on clay tablets. This is found in the library at Nineveh, Assurbanipal. King of Assyria from 668 to 626BC. This event is close to the Genesis account, it gives a flood account, dimensions of a ship. It gives the floor space as about one 'iku' (3,600 sq metres) a height of 120 cubits (55 metres) in seven decks. The flood lasted for seven days. Similarly, a dove and raven are sent out.

Scholars explain the coincidence of the Genesis and Gilgamesh accounts. It has been told that the story was brought from Mesopotamia by Abraham. Some say that it was the Israelites through Armarna, Egypt. Others claim it was at Babylon, at the time of exile. Gilgamesh tablets predate that Assurbanipal ruled 668 to 626BC. The mosaic account claims to be earlier. (Ref Colin Mitchell, Case for Creationism page 163,1994)

The Flood

There have been theories that the flood was caused by prolonged cyclonic storms, but rain could not cause a global flood, these would be classed as uniformitarianism. The flood being local would hold uniformitarianism as being true. The catastrophic view would mean an extra-terrestrial gravitational field on the earth, then the global flood is plausible.

If the flood were local, the flood may have come from one or two regions of the earth, but the flood has accounted for nearly 40 different areas of the hemisphere. Hebrew tradition says that Shem was a survivor of the flood was the oldest man on earth in the patriarchal age, quote from Henry H. Halley's Bible handbook 1959, if Halley's theory is right then Melchizedek is either Shem, Arphaxad, Salah or Eber.

The Hebrews account is that the ark was grounded in the high Ararat-Caucasus-Elburz region. These areas have heights of around 17,000 feet, and 8000 and 10,000 feet above mean sea level. The topography of these areas may give hints to the tides of the flood. There are three lakes of the Armenia region which can be considered at the minimum level at which the ark was grounded. Lake Urmia in Iran is 4,364 ft above sea level. Lake Van in Turkey is 5,620ft, then its Lake Sevan in Russia 6,345 ft. The exact resting place of the ark has not been confirmed. But it's fair to assume it had rested in the vicinity of this area being 8000 feet above sea level. However, the altitude and topography of the Ararat area would meet the conditions for the resting place of the Ark, for tides 10,000 feet and greater, below and above the antediluvian sea level.

If the flood had been caused by atmospheric precipitation, the ark would have floated downwards, and in response solely to the gravity of the earth. (Ref Donald Patten The Biblical Flood, ice Age Epoch page 59, 1970)

If the estimate of compression is 2 tons per sq inch, 300 tons per/sq ft.,

Water 62lbs per cubic ft

10,000 cubic ft water in vertical position is 629,000 lbs of pressure, and is just over 2 tons per sq inch.

(Ref Donald Patten The Biblical Flood, ice Age Epoch page 62, 1970)

With reference to Genesis 7, it says the waters increased and prevailed on the earth, the waters flooded mountains, valleys, plateaus etc., a 'second gravity' which opposes the gravity of the earth has been suggested that caused these tidal upheavals.

Chapter 4

DNA

Psalm 139:13-15 NIV;

'For you created my innermost being. You knit me together in my mother's womb.

I praise you because I am fearfully and wonderfully made; your works are wonderful. I know that full well. My frame was not hidden from you when I was made in the secret place. When I was woven together in the depths of the earth'

The DNA, the deoxyribonucleic acid, is a molecule of two chain coils which coil around each other to form the double-helix carrying a vast amount of information, which is unique to every living organism, consisting of the four nitrogenous bases, Adenine with Thymine, Guanine with Cytosine. These macromolecules are the necessities for life. The DNA is organised into structures called chromosomes The strands of DNA are 5,3 prime on one strand the other is 3,5 prime running the opposite direction. Each of the two strands are nucleotides. The DNA coiled around proteins called histones. Telomeres are repetitive nucleotides at the end of each chromosome.

The DNA assembly uses 20 out of 64 possible sub-assemblies, The basic units are called nucleotides. 15,000 or more atoms are of the individual sub-assemblies. Left to chance by the evolutionary theory, they would go together 10power 87 different ways. 10 billion with 77 more ciphers. Not all the types of sub-assemblies expected at random are available in the same numbers. One of them is more than 10power 61. One can find five more kinds of molecules used in DNA for every 100,000.

R.V. Eck Science 1966, he explains "A mutational change which might be beneficial in one way, in almost every case would be a strong disadvantage in many other ways. When such a mutation occurred, the process of natural selection would therefore reject it". Determination of the sequences of proteins such as ferredoxin and of nucleic acids like transfer RNA, whose prototypes must have functioned at this early time should make possible a detailed reconstruction of the biochemical evolutionary events of this era.

The amoeba, algae or man has a DNA code of the same atomic complexity, with a million atoms of the same arrangement.

F. Crick on the "Genetic Code" Scientific American, 1962, commented on the DNA base nucleotides, the defects are adding or deleting one base, or a small group of them. The addition can be produced at random by compounds called acridines. The resulting changes can be combined and broken up, and there is doubt that they are additions or deletions.

Duane Gish "DNA Its History and Potential" 1967. The simplest code by which 20 amino acids could be specified involves at least three nucleotide pairs or "letters" like ATT, GCA, TCG, ACC, A-adenine, C-cytosine, T-thymine, and G-guanine. The "message" evidently begins at a fixed point at one end of the gene. It is read three bases at a time. If the reading starts at the wrong point, the message will fall into the wrong sets of the three, thus being incorrect. For each correct reading there are two incorrect ones.

A minus with a minus is non-functional. If a plus is combined with a minus close to it, it is restored. The rH region is read correctly or B cistron. The message does not make sense until the minus mutation of the missing base is reached.

If a sequence of three bases is needed to specify an amino acid, 64 could be specified instead of the 20 actually available. Experiments showed that most 64 triplets, codons are not nonsense but stand for amino acids. the rH region is an unimportant function, it was possible to accumulate the large number of mutations, making possible the detailed analysis of this rather minute portion of the T4 phage DNA molecule.(Ref Walter E. Lammerts Why Not Creation page 309)

The virus organism has only one chromosome, as well as man. Algae has many chromosomes. One made of organized proteins and DNA molecules. Evolution geneticists suggest a sort of molecular "polyploidy". They say that bacteria have a single circular chromosome giving rise to two chromosomes. Mutations could then accumulate in the "extra" chromosome. Sexual union or conjugation would occur between two bacteria. The result would be that of a pair of "new" chromosomes. No normal genes.

The Adenine ("A") and the Thymine ("T") both have one donor and one acceptor. The Cytosine ("C") has one donor and two acceptors. The Guanine ("G") has one acceptor and two donors.

10% of your nucleotides in your chromosomes are part of your genes. The remainder are filler nucleotides between genes, i.e. scrambled letters inserted in each sentence, this is also known as junk DNA.

Francis Crick, and James Watson were the scientists who identified the structure of DNA in 1953.

Humans have 46 chromosomes, one half from one parent, and the other from the other parent, 2x 23 chromosomes.

It has been estimated that if the DNA was uncoiled in humans, it would reach the sun and back 300 times. The DNA contains about 200,000 base pairs. Each base pair is one letter of a minimum three letter word, which may specify which of the 20 amino acids is to be linked up into a polypeptide chain. An entire paragraph is needed of such words to specify the sequence of amino acids needed just for one polypeptide chain. Several of these chains are needed for a complex protein.

Typographical errors may occur in the replication of the DNA molecule. Deletions, additions, etc are just some of the examples, and could result in fatal consequences. These errors, mutations can be used to analyze bacteriophage revealing not just the DNA code, but also the cellular activity.

If two mutants, resulting from typographical errors, in different parts of the DNA molecule, some individuals of the standard type will be regenerated, the "crossing-over" occurs. The reconstructed standards will produce plaques on the strain, the original mutants cannot. One can detect a single recombination among billions of offspring. The resolution of two rH mutants are allowed only for one base pair apart in the DNA molecular chain.

It is understood that two defective DNA molecules may actually break apart to form one non-defective molecule. Which is then replicated, or a copy choice, where only the good sections of the two mutant molecules are copied.

If the same kind and number of amino acid molecules were counted out and confined and somehow also protected against "the survival of the fittest" in a thermodynamic equilibrium, there would be a chance out of 10power 31. 10 billion with 21 ciphers added. (Ref Walter E. Lammerts Why Not Creation page 317)

Christian B. Anfinsen on "The Molecular Basis of Evolution" said "We like to believe that Nature has been very wise and efficient in design of the chemical compounds, how large or complicated, which make up the structure of living things" he added "It is unlikely that we shall ever have more opinions regarding the origin of life"

While the DNA of some mammals differs from others by only two of these 20 assemblies, man differs from others by 17.

Dr. Wallace made this insertion on special creation "At the very outset the following point was concluded: any person who is firmly and unalterably convinced that each of today's species of plants and animals arose by an act of special creation, we will find no evidence in Walter E. Lammerts Why NotCreation, that will compel him to change his mind. There is simply no such evidence, nor can there ever be. A Divine Being of infinite wisdom, we must all admit could have created living forms in a manner that we would have dribbled off as by-products all of these things we have gleaned as evidence of evolution. We can only say that He went about His task in a way that mimicked evolution, it is unfortunate that some event did not occur which could have clearly ruled out evolutionary theory.

Dr. Wallace has the concept of ideas that are "untestable", and laws of chance do not provide any proof of a DNA mechanism, to its complexity it is hardly a valid evolutionary process.

F. Crick on the "Genetic Code" Scientific American, 1962, commented on the DNA base nucleotides, the defects are adding or deleting one base, or a small group of them. The addition can be produced at random by compounds called acridines. The resulting changes can be combined and broken up, and there is doubt that they are additions or deletions.

Duane Gish "DNA Its History and Potential" 1967,said ;

' The simplest code by which 20 amino acids could be specified involves at least three nucleotide pairs or "letters" like ATT, GCA, TCG, ACC, A-adenine, C-cytosine, T-thymine, and G-guanine. The "message" evidently begins at a fixed point at one end of the gene. It is read three bases at a time. If the reading starts at the wrong point, the message will fall into the wrong sets of the three, thus being incorrect. For each correct reading there are two incorrect ones.'

A minus with a minus is non-functional. If a plus is combined with a minus close to it, it is restored. The rH region is read correctly or B cistron. The message does not make sense until the minus mutation of the missing base is reached.

If a sequence of three bases is needed to specify an amino acid, 64 could be specified instead of the 20 actually available. Experiments showed that most 64 triplets, codons are not nonsense but stand for amino acids. the rH region is an unimportant function, it was possible to accumulate the large number of mutations, making possible the detailed analysis of this rather minute portion of the T4 phage DNA molecule.(Ref Walter E. Lammerts Why Not Creation page 309)

The virus organism has only one chromosome, as well as man. Algae has many chromosomes. One made of organized proteins and DNA molecules. Evolution geneticists suggest a sort of molecular "polyploidy". They say that bacteria has a single circular chromosome giving rise to two chromosomes. Mutations could then accumulate in the "extra" chromosome. Sexual union or conjugation would occur between two bacteria. The result would be that of a pair of "new" chromosomes. No normal genes.

DNA Research

In 1953, Watson and Crick published their now famous paper in the journal Nature reporting the double helix structure of a then-obscure compound deoxyribonucleic acid.

(Ref Micheal Denton, Evolution, A Theory In Crisis, page 233, 1996).

Kornberg, had discovered the DNA polymerase which an enzyme catalyzes the production of DNA. For this a DNA template is necessary for building blocks (nucleotide forerunners). It should be noted that the resulting polynucleotide (DNA) would not exhibit biological activity like the parent template molecule.

The production of DNA molecules are based on the following factors;

1./ Purification of DNA polymerase

2./Selection of an ideal DNA template

3./ utilization of a polynucleotide-joining enzyme.

By heating carbon dioxide (CO_2) methane (CH_4) ammonia (NH_3) and hydrogen (H_2) in the presence of water energizing the process by electrical discharges or ultraviolet radiation. This process formed products such as hydrogen cyanide (HCN) and formaldehyde (H_2CO).This generated four classes of molecules found in cells: amino acids, nucleotides, sugars, fatty acids. The first two would form polymers, being polypeptides, and polynucleotides. The former are proteins, the others are ribonucleic acids (RNA) and deoxyribonucleic acids (DNA).

It is believed that 1.5 billion years ago, the small prokaryotes gave rise to the more complex eukaryotes.

It is understood that the DNA in a nucleus acts as a template for the production of the RNA, which moves from the nucleus to the surrounding region (cytoplasm) of the cell. The RNA operates as with the ribosomes and dictates the conformation of various proteins, enzymes which are essential for life for the cell and the organism of which the cell is the part.

Types of DNA discovered in various animals, plants, and human cells consists of two strands twisted about each other to form a helical structure. DNA resembles a ladder that has been twisted so that the two sides are spiral-shaped. The strands are joined together at the region of the rings by hydrogen bonds.

2000 atoms in various isotopes of our 100 natural elements, only 10 of these are found in our DNA.

DNA helix is 2 miillimicrons 12 million make 1 inch in the DNA.

Each strand is called a polymer (poly; many, mer; parts) because it is composed of many repeating structural units. Each of these units is a nucleotide, and so each polymeric DNA strand popularity is termed a polynucleotide. All four contain a phosphate group, sugar and a base. The difference resides with the bases, which are named adenine, thymine, cytosine, and guanine. The width of a DNA helix is 2 millimicrons. It would take more than 12 million of these helices side by side to equal one inch.

The DNA becomes a pattern for it's own reproduction at appropriate times, when this happens, the two polynucleotide strands separate. When the reproduction is complete, adenine will join to thymine, cytosine and to guanine. These combinations constitute a four-letter genetic alphabet which is A-T, T-A, C-G, and G-C. Sequence of these letters distinguishes one organism genotypically from all the others. Proteins are formed according to the orders by the arrangement of the letters. (Ref Walter E. Lammerts Why Not Creation page 270)

American biochemist Harold Morowitz speculated the minimum requirements for the self-replicating cell. A minimum of 10 proteins would be required for the synthesis of the nucleotide building blocks for DNA. For the DNA synthesis. Such a cell would also require a protein synthetic apparatus for the synthesis of it's proteins. If this were along the lines of the usual ribosomal system, it would require a minimum of about 80 proteins.

Such a minimal cell contains, say, three ribosomes, 4 mRNA molecules, a full complement of enzymes, a DNA molecule 100,000 nucleotides long and a cell membrane would be about 1000A 1A = 10power8 cm) in diameter.

According to Morowitz:

"This is the smallest hypothetical cell that we can envisage within the context of current biochemical thinking. It is almost certainly a lower limit, since we have allowed no control/functions, no vitamin metabolism and extremely limited intermediary metabolism. Such would be very vulnerable to environmental fluctuation.

Morowitz continues;

"......an average diameter of less than 3000A. Since the minimum hypothetical cell has a diameter of over 1000A, there is a limited gap in which to seek smaller cells".

The minimal cell described above would contain sufficient DNA to code for about one hundred average size proteins, which is close to the observed coding potential of the smallest known bacterial cells. It may be, therefore, that the tiniest of all known bacterial cells are very close to satisfying the minimum criteria for a fully autonomous cell system capable of independent replication.

(Ref Micheal Denton, Evolution, A Theory In Crisis, page 264, 1996)

The rate in all organisms from bacteria to mammals has been estimated for various loci at between 10-9 to 10-10, per base pair copied when DNA is replicated.

(Ref Micheal Denton, Evolution, A Theory In Crisis, page 267, 1996)

Francis Crick, on his book "Life Itself" page 88, 1981, made this comment on the Origin of Life;

"An honest man, armed with all the knowledge available to us now, could only state that in some sense, the origin of life appears at the moment to be almost a miracle, so many are the conditions which would have had to have satisfied to get it going"

(Ref Micheal Denton, Evolution, A Theory In Crisis, page 268, 1996)

For the creation of the first cell, Jacques Monod, biochemist made this comment;

"Life appeared on earth: what, before the event, were the chances that this would occur? The present structure of the biosphere certainly does not exclude the possibility that ..... Its a priori probability was virtually zero".

Francis Crick and L.E> Orgel "Directed Panspermia" pages 341 - 346, 1973. Crick had the idea that life was seeded on earth from space, the idea of panspermia.

Proteins are composed of units known as amino acids; sizes ranging from 50 to 3000 amino acids. It takes 3 nucleotides to determine one amino acid. A production of a chain of 150 amino acids, the nucleotide would need to be a sequence of 450. This sequence is called a gene.

The human body has some 10 trillion cells, each cell has 46 chromosomes in its nucleus. Within the set of chromosomes in each cell, there are around 3 million genes composed of nucleotide pairs of around 5 billion. A single colon of bacterium of Escherichia coli is about ½ micron, (1/50,000 of an inch) wide and two microns long. It has a single chromosome containing a single DNA molecule. The extended DNA molecule is about 1mm long, or 500 times the length of the Escherichia coli cell.

So this complexity does this point to a supernatural designer, or did it occur by chance?. If by chance, we really have to think. The chance of a complicated structure just to happen, seems quite incredible and quite impossible!!!. If it did evolve when and what were the sequences of its evolution. Evidence required!!!

Each of these DNA molecules contains about 10 million nucleotide pairs, which constitute the thousands of genes giving the organism its structure. Genes operate at the same time, each of the functions operate at times in history. The proteins are called histones.

Most plants, animals which began as a single cell, which divides and distributes its DNA equally to all daughter cells. The quantity of DNA in the sex cells would be half the amount of the body cells. The creation of a tiny fruit fly, and all its features would require a proper alignment of 10 millions of polynucleotide pairs in the DNA.

Amino acids are small organic compounds consisting of about 10 to 20 atoms. Each amino acid contains an amino (NH_2) and a carboxylic acid (COOH) group linked by a carbon atom. Some are insoluble in water hydrophobic, some are soluble (hydrophilic) others are acidic.

The amino acids are linked via their amino and carboxyl acid groups to form a long linear polymer which is shown as the primary structure of the protein. The linear sequence of the amino acid in the protein is made up of a combination of 20 amino acid letters. In most proteins the amino acid chain is between 100 and 500 amino acids long.

Every protein has a unique amino acid sequence and this is known as the primary structure.

(Ref Micheal Denton, Evolution, A Theory In Crisis, page 235, 1996).

There are two types of nucleic acids, DNA and RNA. DNA is only found in the nucleus of the cell. (A master). RNA molecules perform the fundamental task of carrying the information stored in the DNA, to all various parts of the cell where the manufacture of a particular protein is proceeding.

The building blocks or subunits of DNA polymers are the nucleotides, each consisting of a phosphate radical, a sugar and a nitrogenous base. There are four nucleotides in DNA and these are linked together to form a long linear polymer. (Ref Micheal Denton, Evolution, A Theory In crisis, page 239, 1996).

Unlike DNA, RNA is a single stranded polymer made up of four nucleotides of very similar chemical structure to those of the DNA. The only difference is that one of the nucleotides of the RNA contains the base uracil instead of thymine. The process of copying the nucleotide sequence of the gene is known as transcription.

At transcription one of the strands of the two strands of the DNA double helix is copied into RNA. One of the helix is unwound and the other directs the synthesis of RNA polymer.

As most genes are about 1000 nucleotides long. Each mRNA molecule, being merely a copy of a gene, consists of a long RNA chain about 1000 nucleotides in length. (Ref Micheal Denton, Evolution,A theory in crisis, page 242, 1996)

Every one of the 64 different nucleotide triplets can be formed from the four nucleotides, A,U,G,C. 61 triplets specified for amino acids. The remaining three happens to be triplets - UAA, UAG, UGA - are used as punctuation signals and mean "stop" indicating the end of a particular message.

After its transcription the mRNA moves from the nucleus into the cytoplasm to the actual site of translation where the decoding of the message takes place.

The translation of the mRNA molecule is carried out by a set of molecules which together form the translational apparatus. A component of the translation is the organelle, the ribosome.

The ribosome is composed of some 50 proteins and three chains of RNA. The ribosome attaches itself to the mRNA at a special site on the mRNA which is known as the ribosome binding site which contains a "Start" triplet AUG, GUG. It is generally close to one end of the mRNA molecule. Each triplet of the RNA to the correct item in the translated message is a particular amino acid. A class of RNA molecules known as transfer or tRNA. Each tRNA molecule consists of a short polymer of RNA and some 100 nucleotides long folded into a compact hairpin loop structure.

During the process of translation the mRNA passes through the ribosome. Proteins in the ribosome remove the amino acid from the tRNA and the amino acid chain is assembled by amino acid, amino acid, as tRNA brings their attached amino acids by the reading head of the ribosome. (Ref Micheal Denton, Evolution, A Theory In Crisis page 245, 1996)

In 1976, Richard Dawkins wrote on the DNA;

'A large fraction of DNA is never translated into protein. From the point of view of the individual organism this seems paradoxical. If the purpose of DNA is to supervise the building of bodies, it is surprising to find a large quantity of DNA which does no such thing.'

DNA Viruses

Viruses in DNA, bacteria carry their DNA in a single stranded condition. Smallpox, Polyoma, T2, T4, T6 have double stranded DNA. Influenza, poliomyelitis,and bacterial virus F2 possess a single RNA strand, Reo viruses have a double-helical form. Genetic information is carried in a single rather than a double nucleotide sequence.

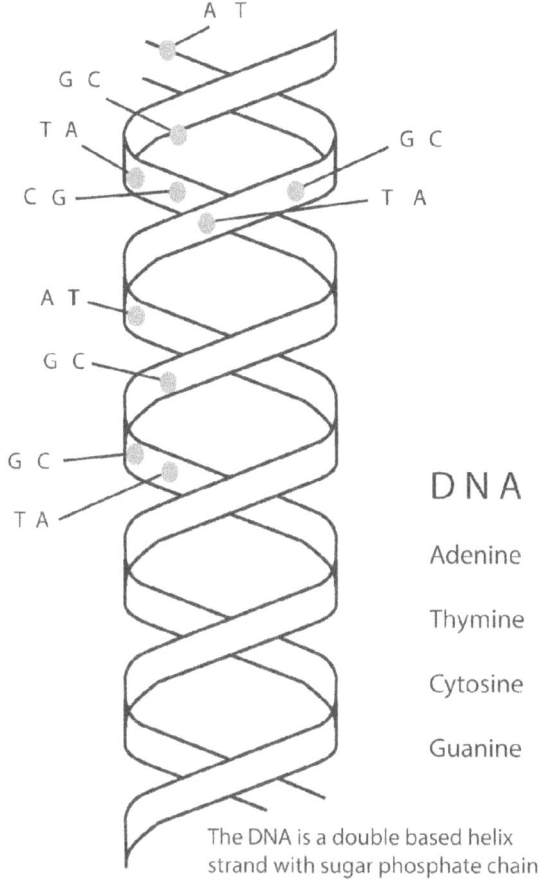

DNA

Adenine

Thymine

Cytosine

Guanine

The DNA is a double based helix strand with sugar phosphate chain

The RNA differs from the DNA, in that at the base it has uracil not thymine.

For a virus to reproduce, they must reproduce its nucleic cell to it's appropriate host cell. If the core is the DNA, the DNA will act as a template for the RNA which works with the cellular machinery like ribosomes and enzymes for producing the viral proteins. The DNA will serve as a template for its own replication.

Viral Activity

From the Escherichia coli, DNA polymerase and polynucleotide-joining-enzyme were obtained and purified. More Escherichia coli cells were broken by a sonic method, the fluid was centrifuged and the supernatant boiled. The supernatant solution therefore, contained the soluble heat-stable heat materials from the bacterial cell.

Stanley Miller described the formation of a variety of organic compounds, this includes amino acids, in an apparatus containing methane, ammonia, hydrogen and water and energized by an electrical discharge. This was evidence that chemical evolution must have occurred. The experiment was not that successful, a selected number of gasses in a closed system and a supplied source of energy. Reduced chemical compounds could not have been produced, in an oxidizing atmosphere, thus being thermodynamically impossible. Philip Abelson of the Geophysical Laboratory of the Institute of Washington stated that the analysis of geological evidence limits the speculation of the nature of the primitive atmosphere and the ocean. The lowest oxidation state possible for carbon was carbon monoxide. Evidence showed that the primitive atmosphere mainly consisted of nitrogen and carbon monoxide, with hydrogen, carbon monoxide, hydrogen, carbon dioxide and water present in lesser qualities. On this basis Miller's experiment did not exist.

A. Oparin in his book "Origin of Life on Earth" commented "Our knowledge of the primary information of the lipids is therefore still scanty and unreliable" and on origins "Certainly it is hard to tell, at present to what extent analogous processes could have taken place under natural conditions independent of organisms." Concerning nucleic acid cells, "the question of the primary, abiogenic substances is however, extremely complicated and poorly understood"

A chemical process, of the polymerization of amino acids at 170 to 180C, G Schramm in 1926, reported that the polymerization of nucleotides when heated with a syrup of polyphosphate ester, results were unconvincing. It has been claimed that chemical evolution took place in "the primordial soup of the primitive oceans" where such high temperatures should be excluded.

G. Howe, has pointed out that a pre-biological earth, without a protective mantle of oxygen and ozone, would have been subjected to heavy doses of radiation in the region of 2,700 to 3,000 angstroms, radiation which breaks C-O, C-H, O-H bonds and others. (Ref Walter E. Lammerts Why Not Creation page 285).

To bridge the gap between the molecular stage of evolution and the cellular. The evolutionist has resorted to the claim that there once existed molecules that were "autocatalytic like the virus". No molecule capable of autocatalytic replication has been discovered. The information necessary for the replication of the protein molecule is believed to be in the gene. This is used to reproduce a messenger RNA. This process requires enzyme systems and energy sources. The amino acids are activated by an intermediate complex with an activating enzyme specific for each amino acid and ATP. This complex reacts with soluble RNA (s-RNA) specific for each amino acid, to give a complex of the amino acid with s-RNA. The AA-s-RNA complexes move to microsomes, where they are laid down in the sequence of by the messenger RNA.

John Cairns commented "The bacterial chromosome has been shown to contain regions concerned solely with the switching on and off the executive actions of outer regions; in turn, these 'operator' genes are controlled by 'regulator' genes.

Such examples like for W.J. Tinkle, his experiments were based on the fruit fly Drosophila, estimated the mean life of a gene to be approx 100,000 years. The favourable gene would be in one in a thousand perhaps. (Ref Walter E. Lammerts Why Not Creation, page 289)

It was suggested that and by B. Commoner in Nature in 1965, that if the development of a creature is governed by DNA. It would be natural to expect the more complicated creature to have the larger amount of DNA. In reality this is not true. Man's cells contain seven picograms of DNA each. African lungfish contain about 100 picograms. Amphiuma , a primitive amphibian, contains 168 picograms. (Ref Walter E. Lammerts Why Not Creation page 295)

It has been said that the formation of DNA is more than the copying of templates. The static specificity of DNA - its nucleotide sequence, is not only regulated by the nucleotide sequence of the template, but also by the specificity of the polymerase enzymes which catalyzes DNA synthesis.

The Synthesis

DNA synthesized has involved the following three, some DNA put in primer, the necessary enzyme, the DNA polymerase and the necessary deoxynucleotides. If the DNA and primer and the enzyme are from the same organisms, the new DNA will be the same as the primer DNA within 5%. If the primer and the enzyme are from separate different organisms, the disparity of sequence of the DNA and the primer DNA would be as 17.25%.

Barry Commoner, a Cellular Biologist commented,

"Self-duplication and biochemical specificity is a property of an intact whole cell, which is an inheritably a complex system, and not the property of one or another molecule"

Commoner also suggested

"The DNA synthesis and the resultant sequestration of the catalytic nucleotides which are active in the oxidation electron transport system will tend to reduce the rate of catabolic degradation of the metabolites. In turn, this may be expected to increase the relative proportion of the available metabolites, which enter into the anabolic process, and thereby contribute to the synthesis of cell substance......one may anticipate a positive correlation between the DNA content and the overall size characteristic of the mature cell and a negative correlation between DNA content and the cell's characteristic rate of oxidative metabolism"

Embryology

So we will discuss the recapitulation theory, the biogenetic law of Ernst Haeckel 'Ontogeny recapitulates phylogeny'.

Haeckel was meaning to say that in embryonic development, the Ontogeny the organism repeats the evolutionary history of the phylum (Phylogeny).

A development which is frequent to embryologists is that the development of the 'gill slits' or the branchial grooves 'gill arches' This supposedly was evidence that at one time man passed through a fish stage. (Ref Genes Genesis and Evolution, John Klotz page 147, 1955)

De Beer, 'Embryology and Evolution' page 60, his comment on the recapitulation theory was;

'The failure to recognise this principle of parallelism of increasing degrees of complexity, this was a grave error in the recapitulation theory'

He continued with this statement on embryology; 'Any degree with ancestral types. He believes that embryology may give some indication of affinity.

'The descendant may be derived from a larval form of the ancestor, and in such case the resemblance between the young form of the descendant, may conform little or no information concerning the adult form of the ancestor' (Ref Genes Genesis and Evolution, John Klotz page 152, 1955)

Huxley believes that for species the female produces more eggs, though this cannot for the development of display characteristics, if this was so, the male who developed the behaviour patterns characterizing courtship display could not have been favoured. Huxley says it has become clear that the hypothesis of the female choice and the selection between male rivals is irrespective of general biological advantage. (Ref Genes Genesis and Evolution, John Klotz page 175, 177, 1955)

Houseflies

It is estimated that the DNA contains about 200,000 base pairs. Each base pair is one letter of a minimum three letter word, which may specify which of the 20odd amino acids is to be linked up into a polypeptide chain. An entire paragraph is needed of such words to specify the sequence of amino acids needed just for one polypeptide chain. Several of these chains are needed for a complex protein.

Typographical errors may occur in the replication of the DNA molecule. Deletions, additions, etc are just some of the examples, and could result in fatal consequences. These errors, mutations can be used to analyze bacteriophage revealing not just the DNA code, but also the cellular activity.

If two mutants, resulting from typographical errors, in different parts of the DNA molecule, some individuals of the standard type will be regenerated, the "crossing-over" occurs. The reconstructed standards will produce plaques on the strain, the original mutants cannot. One can detect a single recombination among billions of offspring. The resolution of two rH mutants are allowed only for one base pair apart in the DNA molecular chain.

It is understood that two defective DNA molecules may actually break apart to form one non-defective molecule. Which is then replicated, or a copy choice, where only the good sections of the two mutant molecules are copied.

The DNA assembly uses 20 out of 64 possible sub-assemblies, The basic units are called nucleotides. 15,000 or more atoms are of the individual sub-assemblies. Left to chance by the evolutionary theory, they would go together 10^{87} different ways. 10 billion with 77 more ciphers. Not all the types of sub-assemblies expected at random are available in the same numbers. One of them is more than 10^{61}. One can find five more kinds of molecules used in DNA for every 100,000.

If the same kind and number of amino acid molecules were counted out and confined and somehow also protected against "the survival of the fittest" in a thermodynamic equilibrium, there would be a chance out of 10^{31}. 10 billion with 21 ciphers added. (Ref Walter E. Lammerts Why Not Creation page 317)

Christian B. Anfinsen on "The Molecular Basis of Evolution" said "We like to believe that Nature has been very wise and efficient in design of the chemical compounds, how large or complicated, which make up the structure of living things" he added "It is unlikely that we shall ever have more opinions regarding the origin of life"

While the DNA of some mammals differs from others by only two of these 20 assemblies, man differs from others by 17.

F. Crick on the "Genetic Code" Scientific American, 1962, commented on the DNA base nucleotides, the defects are adding or deleting one base, or a small group of them. The addition can be produced at random by compounds called acridines. The resulting changes can be combined and broken up, and there is doubt that they are additions or deletions.

Duane Gish "DNA Its History and Potential" 1967. The simplest code by which 20 amino acids could be specified involves at least three nucleotide pairs or "letters" like ATT, GCA, TCG, ACC, A-adenine, C-cytosine, T-thymine, and G-guanine. The "message" evidently begins at a fixed point at one end of the gene. It is read three bases at a time. If the reading starts at the wrong point, the message will fall into the wrong sets of the three, thus being incorrect. For each correct reading there are two incorrect ones.

A minus with a minus is non-functional. If a plus is combined with a minus close to it, it is restored. The rH region is read correctly or B cistron. The message does not make sense until the minus mutation of the missing base is reached.

If a sequence of three bases is needed to specify an amino acid, 64 could be specified instead of the 20 actually available. Experiments showed that most 64 triplets, codons are not nonsense but stand for amino acids. the rH region is an unimportant function, it was possible to accumulate the large number of mutations, making possible the detailed analysis of this rather minute portion of the T4 phage DNA molecule.(Ref Walter E. Lammerts Why Not Creation page 309)

The virus organism has only one chromosome, as well as man. Algae has many chromosomes. One made of organized proteins and DNA molecules. Evolution geneticists suggest a sort of molecular "polyploidy". They say that bacteria has a single circular chromosome giving rise to two chromosomes. Mutations could then accumulate in the "extra" chromosome. Sexual union or conjugation would occur between two bacteria. The result would be that of a pair of "new" chromosomes. No normal genes.

G.G. Simpson explained on the nature and development of DNA and stated;

"In due course molecular biology will undoubtedly become more firmly connected with the biology of the whole organisms of evolution, and then will be a greater concern for those more interested in the nature of man, than in the nature of molecules." (Ref G.G. Simpson, Science 1966)

R.V. Eck Science 1966, he explains;

"A mutational change which might be beneficial in one way, in almost every case would be a strong disadvantage in many other ways. When such a mutation occurred, the process of natural selection would therefore reject it". Determination of the sequences of proteins such as ferredoxin and of nucleic acids like transfer RNA, whose prototypes must have functioned at this early time should make possible a detailed reconstruction of the biochemical evolutionary events of this era.

The amoeba, algae or man has a DNA code of the same atomic complexity, with a million atoms of the same arrangement.

G.G. Simpson explained the nature and development of DNA and stated "In due course molecular biology will undoubtedly become more firmly connected with the biology of the whole organisms of evolution, and then will be a greater concern for those more interested in the nature of man, than in the nature of molecules." (Ref G.G. Simpson, Science 1966)

R.V. Eck Science 1966, he explains "A mutational change which might be beneficial in one way, in almost every case would be a strong disadvantage in many other ways. When such a mutation occurred, the process of natural selection would therefore reject it". Determination of the sequences of proteins such as ferredoxin and of nucleic acids like transfer RNA, whose prototypes must have functioned at this early time should make possible a detailed reconstruction of the biochemical evolutionary events of this era.

The amoeba, algae or man has a DNA code of the same atomic complexity, with a million atoms of the same arrangement.

G.G. Simpson explained the nature and development of DNA and stated "In due course molecular biology will undoubtedly become more firmly connected with the biology of the whole organisms of evolution, and then will be a greater concern for those more interested in the nature of man, than in the nature of molecules." (Ref G.G. Simpson, Science 1966)

Haemoglobin

Snake like objects are formed from about 150 amino acids in a spiral fashion. At one point on each chain these are attached by a histidine link to form as plate shaped haem units which consist of iron atoms surrounded by four pyrrole rings. Oxygen molecules attach to the reverse side of these plates. The whole molecule fitting one to another is ball-shaped. (Ref Robert E.D. Clark, The Universe, Plan or Accident, page 137, 1961)

The evolutionary biologist Ernst Mayr and his publication 'Systematics and The Origin of Species' 1942. Mayr agreed with Darwin's definition and claimed;

'In determining whether a form should be ranked as a specimen or a variety, the opinion of naturalists.

having sound judgement and wide experience seems the only guide to follow.'

A report by Micheal Marshall a journalist of Forbes Science magazine, where he says that the human race was reduced to a population of two, and then repopulated the planet was wrong be based this on the;

1./Mitochondrial DNA, Marshall says the Mitochondrial DNA is only inherited from the mother.giving information only of the female line?.

2./ Extinctions from humans?

3./ No geological record in any global event in the last 200,000 years?

It has been explained by the "Housefly Resistance to Insecticides" C.P. Georghiou, this was his comment;

"It is now well established that the development of increased ability in insects to survive exposure is not induced directly by the insecticides themselves. These chemicals do not cause the genetic changes in insects; they only serve as selective agents, eliminating the more susceptible insects and enabling the more tolerant survivors to increase and fill the void created by destruction of susceptible individuals".

It is estimated that the DNA contains about 200,000 base pairs. Each base pair is one letter of a minimum three letter word, which may specify which of the 20 odd amino acids is to be linked up into a polypeptide chain. An entire paragraph is needed of such words to specify the sequence of amino acids needed just for one polypeptide chain. Several of these chains are needed for a complex protein.

Typographical errors may occur in the replication of the DNA molecule. Deletions, additions, etc are just some of the examples, and could result in fatal consequences. These errors, mutations can be used to analyze bacteriophage revealing not just the DNA code, but also the cellular activity.

If two mutants, resulting from typographical errors, in different parts of the DNA molecule, some individuals of the standard type will be regenerated, the "crossing-over" occurs. The reconstructed standards will produce plaques on the strain, the original mutants cannot. One can detect a single recombination among billions of offspring. The resolution of two rH mutants are allowed only for one base pair apart in the DNA molecular chain.

It is understood that two defective DNA molecules may actually break apart to form one non-defective molecule. Which is then replicated, or a copy choice, where only the good sections of the two mutant molecules are copied.

The DNA assembly uses 20 out of 64 possible sub-assemblies, The basic units are called nucleotides. 15,000 or more atoms are of the individual sub-assemblies. Left to chance by the evolutionary theory, they would go together 10^{87} different ways. 10 billion with 77 more ciphers. Not all the types of sub-assemblies expected at random are available in the same numbers. One of them is more than 10^{61}. One can find five more kinds of molecules used in DNA for every 100,000.

If the same kind and number of amino acid molecules were counted out and confined and somehow also protected against "the survival of the fittest" in a thermodynamic equilibrium, there would be a chance out of 10^{31}. 10 billion with 21 ciphers added. (Ref Walter E. Lammerts Why Not Creation page 317)

Christian B. Anfinsen on "The Molecular Basis of Evolution" said "We like to believe that Nature has been very wise and efficient in design of the chemical compounds, how large or complicated, which make up the structure of living things" he added "It is unlikely that we shall ever have more opinions regarding the origin of life"

While the DNA of some mammals differs from others by only two of these 20 assemblies, man differs from others by 17.

Chapter 5

Good Mutations for Evolution

Parallel Mutations a classic example would be the fruit flies Drosophila Melanogaster and Drosophila Simulans.

Homologous and analogous structures ;

Homologous are structures that correspond one to another, but not necessarily having the same function.

Analogous are structures that have the same function, but do not correspond to each other. This could be a bird wing and one of a bat. They perform the same function which could be analogous, but not regarded as homologous.

Parallel Mutations a classic example would be the fruit flies Drosophila Melanogaster and Drosophila Simulans.

Homologous and analogous structures ;

Homologous are structures that correspond one to another, but not necessarily having the same function.

Analogous are structures that have the same function, but do not correspond to each other. This could be a bird wing and one of a bat. They perform the same function which could be analogous, but not regarded as homologous.

August Weiseman in 1892, in his germ plasm theory, "Das Keimplasma". He showed that reproductive cells assembled from various parts of the body, and formed a continuous line from generation to generation, developing from germinal tissue. The somatic cells were then the result of germ cell activity.

His theory was correct that chromosomes carry genes or factors determining the character of the body, and they are protected during cell division and gamete formation. (Ref Walter E. Lammerts Why Not Creation, page 251)

Cytochrome

No animal cytochrome is an intermediate between animals and the other 2 eucaryote groups.

Cytochrome C varied less between species than haemoglobin;

The haemoglobin sequences of man and dog differed by 20%, but the Cytochrome sequences varied by 5%.

The haemoglobin sequences of man and carp varied by 50%, but the Cytochrome sequences varied by 13%.

(Ref Micheal Denton, Evolution, A Theory in Crisis, page 276, 1996)

All cytochrome C molecules are about one hundred amino acids long. A taxonomic distance increases, example between a horse and a dog (two mammals) the divergence is 6%, between a horse and a turtle (two vertebrates) the divergence is 11%., between the horse and fruit fly (two animals) the divergence is 22%. (Ref Micheal Denton, Evolution, A Theory In Crisis, page 278, 1996).

There are no intermediates to bridge the gap between procaryotes and eucaryotes.

(Ref Micheal Denton, Evolution, A theory in crisis, page 281, 1996)

Haemoglobin differs by 50% between man and carp, the cytochrome C differs by 13%.

The Haemoglobin sequences of a particular group differ from 50%, all cytochrome C sequences differ about 13%. It is necessary for evolutionary theory to presume that the molecular clock has ticked a faster rate in haemoglobin than in the case of cytochrome C.

The two types of changes that can occur to the sequence of the genes specifying functional proteins: **Neutral Mutations**, these have no effect on function and are substituted by drift; and are **advantageous mutations,** that have a positive effect on function and are substituted by selection.

J.W.Ewens "Comments on Dr. Kimura's Paper" Genetics said;

"I note the well known fact that the neutral theory predicts a constant rate of substitution per generation, whereas we appear to observe more a constant rate per year. In some of the species for which protein sequence comparisons have been made, there is a difference of one or even two orders of magnitude in generation time. It surely gets us nowhere simply to assume that the mutation rate adjusts itself in species of different generation time so that constant rates per year will arise."

(Ref Micheal Denton, Evolution, A Theory In Crisis, page 298, 1996)

For commentary on haemoglobin E, Zukerkandl on "The Evolution of Haemoglobin" pages 110 t0 118, 1965, made the following comments;

"Contemporary organisms that look much like ancient ancestral organisms probably contain a majority of polypeptide chains that resemble quite closely those of the ancient organisms. In other words, certain animals said to be "living fossils", such as the cockroach, the horseshoe crab, the shark and, among mammals, the lemur, probably manufacture a great many polypeptide molecules that differ only slightly from those manufactured by their ancestors millions of years ago."

Parallel Mutations

There could be evidence that of descent from a common ancestor, a slight modification is observed. Individuals who resemble each other are closely related by descent. Identical twins are an example, for the common ancestor this may go further back to the distant past, evidence of this is the phenomena of parallel mutations. Drosophila Melanogaster, Drosophila Simulans have experienced mutations of eye colour, body colour, and wings. It is suggested that the phenomena of parallel mutations is a case for evolution (Ref., Walter E. Lammerts his book, Why Not Creation 1970).

Dobzhansky quotes from his book, 'Evolution of Genes and Genes in Evolution 'But here is a great caveat: phenotypically similar, or mimetic mutants are also produced different, fully complementary and not even linked genes within a species. Among the classic mutants in Drosophila Melanogaster there are changes of eye colour, eye surface. Of these few mimetic genes may conceivably have arisen through the reduplication of the same ancestral genes. But for the majority such a supposition is quite gratuitous. Our powers of observation are limited, and what to our eyes are phenotypically similar changes may actually be due to different genes.'

Dobzhansky said ' The presence of homologous organs is, then, not necessarily evidence of persistence of identical, similar, or even homologous genes. The genetic system which brings about the development of an eye in a fish is probably quite different from that of an eye in a bird or in a man'.

He also said, "What has been said above the concerning organs applies as well as to their chemical constituents and to enzymes. To an evolutionist, the fact that certain enzymes are widely distributed in most diverse organisms are very impressive. But to conclude that these chemical constituents are produced everywhere by the same genes is going far beyond what is justified by the evidence."

Chromosomal changes, chromosomal aberrations, gene mutations for variations, Darwin considered that variations in organisms by natural selection were selecting the fit, killing those that were unfit. Chromosomal changes have a slight chance of survival because they upset a great deal the delicate balance of the gene complex. Polyploidy had the greatest possibility of survival. (Ref. Walter E. Lammerts, Why Not Creation 1969). It has been claimed that Polypoids succumb because they cannot go back to the diploid condition, their gradual change of genetic variation seems to be hampered by the high number of chromosomes (Ref Thomas Cameron, Evolution Its Science and Doctrine 1960).

According to Ehrlich and Holm, Polypoids are extremely common in plants and animals, then they must result in a selective advantage, (circular reasoning). Aneuploidy, however, is deadly to the chromosome number, causing it to decrease. (Ref Walter E Lammerts, Why Not Creation 1969).

A major problem with mutations is that most are lethal, and are not favourable to evolution. It was calculated that out of 10,000 mutations, which have 1% of selective advantage, 9,803 will be eliminated. Therefore in 10,000 mutations, 197 can expect to survive. (Ref Walter E. Lammerts, Why Not Creation 1969)

Mutation Rates

It is believed that mutations take place in the order of 10^{-5} (.0001) or 10^{-6} (.000001) per reproductive cell per generation. Because a given character is affected by a number of genes, it is believed that the frequency of new mutations affecting a single character may be in the order of 10^{-4} (.0001) or 10^{-2} (.01). 14. It is estimated that in Drosophila on the basis of mutation rate of 10^{-6} a given gene will mutate once in about 40,000 years.. It is believed that one in every 20 germ cells will contain some sort of mutation. (Ref John Klotz, Genes Genesis and Evolution page 279)

Penrose and Haldane estimated that the normal allele of the hemophilia gene mutates to hemophilia about once in 50 to 100,000 individuals per generation.It is believed that the "X" chromosomes mutates 10 times as frequently than the "X" chromosome of the female.

An estimation of mutation frequency of man, (Neal and Falls) It was suggested by them that man has 20,000 gene loci, and if the average mutation rate is 2.6×10^{-5} then the average mutation rate is ($2.6 \times 10^{-2} \times 2 \times 10$ power of 4. This is such that each diploid individually possesses one mutant gene not present in either parent.

Muller's figure on the frequency of mutation is 0.1 to 0.5 per diploid individual compared with the 1.0 suggested by Neal and Falls. (Ref J.H Muller "Our Load of Mutations" 1947) and J.Neel and F.Falls "The Rate of Mutation Of the Gene Responsible for Retinoblastoma in Man" 1951.

Timofeeff-Ressovsky suggests a lower rate. He believed the total mutation rate per generation is of the magnitude of from 1 to 10%, being a rate of 0.01 to 0.1 per diploid individual. (Ref Timofeeff-Ressovsky N.W. "Mutations and Geographical Variation" 1940)

Winchester believed that the mutation rate of man is less than 10% than of Drosophila,

Julian Huxley 'Evolution in Action, page 144, 1953, his calculations of H.J. Mueller;

Stated the chance of getting a horse from a single-celled organism by mutation without natural selection is one chance out of 10 power 3,000,000.

Huxley is saying that getting a horse by mutation, without natural selection would be impossible, though he says it's happened. The Mutation rate is dependent on the wavelength.

Huxley said that 'no one holds any longer to the notion that species in higher animals arise by a single mutation or even a few steps. Evolution he says consists in the accumulation and integration of many and small genetic changes. The direct and complete proof of the utilization of mutations in evolution under natural conditions has not yet been given.

George Gaylord Simpson 'Tempo Mode in Evolution' 1944 page 54. He stated;

'It has been calculated, that if the mutation rate were 0.0001 (1 in 100,000 an average mutation rate) The probability would be that 5 simultaneous mutations would occur in any one individual would be 1×10 power 22. This would mean that if the populated average 100,000,000 individuals and if the average generation lasted but one day. Such an event appearance of 5 simultaneous mutations in one individual would be expected once in every 274 billion years!'

(Ref Genes Genesis Evolution John Klotz page 298, 1955)

Charles Elton 'Animal Numbers and Adaptation Evolution' 1938 page 134.

Elton believes that the mutation rates do not seem to be sufficient to account without a discriminate spread of the origin ecologically of the adaptive features in species.

Catastrophic Selection

The discovery that strains of bacteria, resistant to penicillin, etc., showed the effects that they were to cure various diseases, and this was proof that beneficial mutations did occur.

This however, did not mean that mutations occurred as a result of penicillin, rather they occurred at a constant rate. Associated with the resistance, there is always a decrease in viability under normal conditions. Under these normal conditions they are soon "swamped out". They are either completely eliminated or are carried as heterozygotes in a small number of bacteria. Heterozygosity does not occur in bacteria.

When a strain is exposed to antibiotics, either the mutation rate, or the defective resistant mutations is so high, that sooner or later one occurs, the entire population has a resistant type in which new medication is necessary.

Chromosomes

Genes arranged in linear order in structure are known as chromosomes. Chromosomes are not found in nesting cells. The highest chromosome number is that of a protozoan, single cell radiolarian with 1600 chromosomes. The homologous chromosomes are paired chromosomes. Sex chromosomes in paired condition in man sre homogametic or 'xx' this produces the female and the unpaired heterogametic 'xy'.

(Ref Genes Genesis and Evolution, page 272 John Klotz, 1955)

Cause of Mutations

The majority of mutations have been produced by X-ray. Organisms are exposed to a measured number of roentgen units and then bred. (Ref C.P.Oliver "The Effect of Varying the Duration of X-Ray Treatment Upon the Frequency of Mutation" 1930). The mutation rate is independent of the wavelength.

Natural radiation cannot be an agent to cause mutations. Cosmic rays from outer space are not abundant enough to cause a mutation rate. (Ref John Klotz, Genes Genesis and Evolution page 282)

Favourable Mutations

Some mutations like in the purple eye and arc wing occur together in Drosophila, the viability rate is increased. Both "purple" and "arc" alone reduce the viability rate, so that the flies with either of these mutations have a lower viability rate than the wild flies. Though, when both are combined in a single individual the viability rate is increased. This increase does not bring viability to wild type flies. The results for male and females had a life span of 39.47 +- 0.28 days. The purple flies had a life span of 24.54 +- 18 days."Purple Arc" combination increased life span to 33.71 +- 0.34 days.

Another mutation that is supposed to be favourable is one which abolishes phototropism.,note by McEwen in 1918. Where Drosophila flies toward a light then changes colour. It has not been confirmed that the effects are favourable genes. Timofeeff-

Ressovsky in the New Systematics mentions two mutants and one combination of mutants in Drosophila funebris which result in a viability of a higher type.

(Ref John Klotz Genes, Genesis and Evolution pages 283, 284)

Ford believes that beneficial mutations occur once in every 1,000,000,000 individuals. (Ref E.B. Ford Mendelism and Evolution 1949, page 46) .J.H. Muller "The Method of Evolution" 1929, page 488, states the vast majority of observed mutations are positively detrimental. This idea supports Darwin.

Ford also stated that the production of small superficial differences, or with obvious pathological departures that in normal condition could not, in any event survive in nature. Ford said that no mutation has ever occurred in the process of genetic work, which is fully viable and which behaves as a dominant wild gene type. 197 out of 10,000 favourable genes with a survival advantage , 1% will survive if the mutation is favourable, if not it will be eliminated.

(Ref Genes Genesis Evolution John Klotz, page 286,294 1955)

Cecil Gordon "An Experiment on a Released Population of D. Melongaster 1935, page 381. He liberated 36,000 Drosophila melanogaster in the UK. The population contained 50% of a recessive gene ebony. 25% were type, 25% were homozygous "ebony" and 50% were homozygous. After 120 days a period of five generations,it was found that the frequency of recessive had fallen to 11%."

Ford also said that no mutation has ever occurred in the progress of genetic work which is fully viable and which behaves as a dominant to the wild type gene.

J.H. Muller says that most mutations in Drosophila are reversible. Often the reverse mutation appears to reconstitute precisely the original gene.

Huxley reports that in guinea pigs a stock developed with four toes on its hind feet. Normal guinea pigs have only three toes on their hind feet. It is believed they evolved from a four toe stock, and lost it's fourth toe million of years ago.

Position Effects of Genes

The effect of the gene is changed by its surrounding of different genes. The normal sequence of genes is ABCDEF gene "C" has a certain effect. If the sequence is altered by a chromosomal arrangement, the sequence then becomes ABCDEFG, the effect of the gene "C" will be different.

The fundamental units inherited are genes. These are tiny structures found in the nucleus in every cell. The gene size ranges from the size of a small virus to a size of a molecule.

Selective Value of Mutations

It is believed that the smaller the mutations, the less likely it is to upset the balance of the gene complex, and the more likely it is to be favourable in toto. It is known as the coefficient of selection, and it is calculated as. Gene "A" and it's allele "a " should occur in the same number of individuals in each generation, assuming the frequency of the two genes in the general population is the same. If the selection favours "A" over "a" they will not continue to be frequent, but "A" will become more common than "a". In the generation following the one in which they are equally frequent, "A" will occur in n individuals, and "a" will occur in (l-s) n individuals. The s is the coefficient favouring "A". (Ref John Klotz, Genes, Genesis and Evolution pages 292, 293)

Fisher calculated, the chance of survival of a given genes was illustrated in the table below;

Number of Generations	No Advantage	s = 0.01
1	0.6321	0.6358
3	0.3741	0.3803
7	0.2095	0.2175
15	0.1127	0.1217
31	0.0589	0.0687
63	0.0302	0.0409
127	0.0153	0.0271
Limit	0.0000	0.0197

It can be stated that 197 out of the favourable 10,000 genes with a survival advantage of 1% will survive. The probability is that even if the mutation is slightly favourable it will be eliminated. Fisher claims;

That even if a mutation confers with some quality, the chances are strongly against its survival in the species.

Coefficients of .01 corresponding to the 1% advantage in the above table are explained. Wright believes that most of the mutations have been important in evolution have had a much smaller selective coefficient, than it is practical. (Ref Sewall Wright "The Statistical Consequences of Mendelian Heredity in Relation to Speciation" 1940, page 178.. This means that fewer than 197 of the 10,000 favourable mutations will survive.

It is reported by Boyd, that a dominant gene, had a selective advantage of 0.1%, it's frequency in the stock would increase from 5% to 50%, in slightly less than 3000 generations, a period corresponding to between 60,000 to 70,000 years in man. In all this time it would have resulted in a new species. It would have been as common as the population as it's allele. This assumes frequency at the beginning of 5%. (Ref John Klotz, Genes, Genes and Evolution, page 295).

The table below reports the time required to a given change per frequency of a gene having a selective advantage of 0.01 (1 %).

Dominant Gene Change in Generations	No. of Frequency from Generations	Recessive Gene Change in Generations	No. of Generations
0.01 - 0.1	230	0.01 - 0.1	900,230
0.1 - 1.0	231	0.1 - 1.0	90,231
1.0 - 50.0	559	1.0 - 3.0	6,779
50.0 - 97.0	3,481	3.0 - 50.0	3,481
97.0 - 99.0	6,779	50.0 - 99.0	99.0 -
231	99.9	90,231	99.0 - 99.9

This means that a gene having a selective advantage of 1%, and this is a greater advantage than most mutations which Wright believes have been important in evolution have had, would completely replace its allele in somewhat more than 1,001,741 generations. For the gene to gain equality with it's allele would take 1,020 generations if the gene were dominant, and 1,000,721 generations if the gene were recessive. (Ref John Klotz, Genes, Genesis and Evolution page 295)

Carter says that the rate is so slow in recessives that as long as the mutation is rare, it is doubtful if it is fast enough to give a basis of differentiation. He also states some recessives may develop into dominants.

Carter believes that a recessive gene with a selective advantage of 0.1% would increase in frequency a population from 0.001% to 1% in 309,780 generations. It would go from 1% to 50% in 11,624 generations, from 50% to 99% in 4,819 generations, from 99% to 99.999% in 6,920 generations. The speed of the spread of a dominant would be the opposite.

Sewall Wright produced calculations on the table below.

Population Homozygous Recessive 0.01	Advantage Of (Neutral Gene)	No Advantage Homozygous Recessive 0.01	Disadvantage O Size
10	0.05	0.05	0.05
50	0.013	0.01	0.007
200	0.0057	0.0025	0.0003
800	0.0027	0.0006	0.00000

It has been calculated that if the mutation rate were .00001 (1 in 100,000 - an average mutation rate) and if the occurrence of each mutation doubled the chance of another mutation occurring in the same cell, the probability that five simultaneous mutations would occur in any one individual would be 1 x 10 power 22. It would mean that if the population averaged 100,000,000 individuals and if the average generation lasted but one day, such an event (the appearance of five simultaneous mutations in one individual) would be expected once in every 274 billion years. (Ref John Klotz, Genes Genesis and Evolution page 297 to 298)

Sewall Wright 'Statistical Consequences of Mendelian History in Relation to Speciation' 1940 page 178.

Wright believes that most of the mutations have been important in evolution, though they have had a smaller selective coefficient, than it is practical to demonstrate in a laboratory. Therefore, 197 out of 10,000 mutations will not survive.

(Ref Genes Genesis Evolution, John klotz, page 294 1955)

Boyd reported that if a dominant gene had an advantage of 0.1% then its frequency in the stock would increase from 5% to 50% in slightly less than 3000 generations (a period of 60 to 70,000 years in man). By this time it not only could form a new species but it could have been as common in the population as it's allele. It really means that a gene having a selective advantage of 1%, would completely replace its allele in more than 1001,in 741 generations.

(Ref Genes Genesis Evolution John Klotz page 295, 1955)

G.S. Carter believed that a recessive gene, with a selective advantage of 0.1%, would increase the frequency in a population from 0.001% to 1% in 309,780 generations. It would go from 1% to 50% in 11,624 generations.

1% to 50% in 11,624 generations

50% to 99% in 4,819 generations

99% to 99.999% in 6,920 generations.

The speed of the dominant would be the opposite;

It would go from 0.001% to 1% 6,920 generations. 1% in 4,819 generations.

(Ref Genes Genesis Evolution John Klotz page 295, 1955)

Reverse Mutations

Dollo's law stated that evolution is irreversible. Though it is believed that evolution is reversible. Romer says that there is evidence of reversibility of evolution and the paleontological evidence is conclusive. He believes that the idea of irreversibility of evolution can no longer be accepted.

J.H. Muller "Reversibility in Evolution from the Standpoint of Genetics" 1939, states that most mutations of Drosophila are reversible in the direction and that very often the reverse mutation appears to reconstitute precisely the original gene. Huxley reports that in guinea pigs a stock has been developed with four toes on the hind feet. The normal guinea pig has three toes on its hind feet. It is believed to have evolved from a four-toed stock and to have lost its fourth toe millions of years ago.

The development of the fourth toe is believed by Huxley to indicate that reverse evolution may occur. (Ref John Klotz, Genes Genesis and Evolution page 299).

J.H. Muller 'Our Load of Mutations' 1950 page 169, he claimed that, the frequency of mutation is 0.1 to 0.5 per diploid individual.

Muller concludes that real reversibility in evolution does not occur. Blum doubts that the mutations reported are strictly reversible changes., Muller believes the reverse mutations often reconstitute the original gene.

It is believed that recessive genes in the autosomes do not exert their effects except when homozygous (occurring in a double dose) This cannot occur unless two individuals are heterozygous (carrying one dominant and one recessive gene). R.A. Fisher ``The Measurement of Selective Intensity" 1936, page 39 explains, the explanatory content of a theory of evolution only reaches zero with the mutation theory.

Huxley says, No one holds any longer to the notion that species of higher animals arise by a single mutation or even in a few steps. Evolution, he believes consists of the accumulation and integration of many and mainly small genetic changes. Huxley also says that the direct and complete proof of the utilization of mutations in evolution under natural conditions has not been given.

Hooton believes there are problems in a theory of multiple spontaneous variations transmitted by heredity and miraculously selected through surviving generations in such a way as to simulate direct morphological adaptation. He says that a complete dependence upon such a theory of evolution involves incredible absurdities. (Ref Earnest Albert Hooton "Up From The Ape" 1946, page77)

Lindsey believes that evolution is scarcely logical to believe that it has come as a result of haphazard genetic changes or random mutations with an assumed preadaptive value. (Ref Arthur Ward Lindsey "Principles of Organic Evolution" 1952, page 346)

Goldschmidt is outspoken in his condemnation of mutations as a mechanism for evolution. He believes at most they can bring about changes within the species. The subspecies, varieties formed are neither incipient species nor models for the origin of species. (Ref Richard Goldschmidt. "The Natural Basis of Evolution" 1940, page 183)

Homology

In homology the detailed comparison of structure after structure in different organisms.

Biologists have made the distinction between homologous and analogous structures.

Homologous; structures are those that correspond one to another, but not necessarily have the same function.

Analogous structures have the same function, but do not correspond to each other, an example of this is the wing of a bird, and a wing of a bat. They perform the same function, but do not correspond to each other.

The woolly rhinoceros, extinct and the woolly rhinoceros which have similar tooth and skull structure, though it is believed that they are not closely related as the fossil evidence indicates they came from different ancestors. Evolutionists believe they evolved parallely, since the Miocene and Pliocene eras.

(Ref Genes Genesis and Evolution John Klotz page 130, 1955)

Chromosomes

Genes arranged in a linea order in structure are known as chromosomes. Chromosomes are not found in nesting cells.. The highest number in a protozoan single-cell radiolarion is 1600 units of chromosomes.

(Ref Genes, Genesis Evolution page 272, John Klotz 1955)

Homologous chromosomes are paired chromosomes. Autosomes are sex chromosomes.

Sex chromosomes in paired condition in man are homogametic or 'xx'. This produces the female and the unpaired heterogametic 'xy'.

Higher chromosome numbers in species have been built up by a process called amphidiploid. When discussing this it should be taken into account what is meant by the term "species". Jean Clausen said that ecotypes or genetic physiological races. Genes of two ecospecies cannot freely interchange genes without impairing the vitality of the hybrid offspring. Cenospecies are unable to exchange genes with one another. Chromosomes do not form pairs, but may produce hybrids. Crossing of Cenospecies with the doubling of the chromosome number, amphidiploid may occur. (Ref Walter E.Lammerts Why Not Creation page 255)

When amphidiploids were first produced "It was tacitly assumed that simple doubling of the chromosome number would render any sterile hybrid fertile and vigorous" (Ref Jens Clausen "Experimental Studies on the Nature of Species" 1945) Cytogenetic research showed this is not true.

One famous was the Raphanobrassica hybrid, produced by Karpenchenko in 1927 "Polyploid Hybrids of Raphanus Sativus". A uniform F3 population was obtained, all 36 plants being quite fertile had 2n = 36 chromosomes.

Richaria and Howard in "Fertility of Amphidiploids" 1937, made some studies of hybrids, the F1 hybrids formed a variable number of bivalents at the reduction division, usually 2 to 3% per cell. Many of the F2 plants had less than 36 chromosomes, those with 36 showed variable pairing with univalents and quadrivalents occuring. 17 to 19 chromosomes were found in the pollen mother cell and accordingly even in the F4 plants varied in the chromosome number from 33 to 37 chromosomes. The F2 plants were only partially fertile and in the F4 fertility varied from 5 to 42%.

Another amphidiploid the Galeopsis artificial Tetrahit by Arne Muntzing, Galeopsis pubescens by Galeopsis speciosa, these showed some chromosome homology. 5 of the 8 pairs of the chromosomes were observed at the reduction division. Diploid F2 generation of 197 plants was grown.

Plants C. japonica with C. reticulata had 45 pairs of chromosomes, which was a result of a diploid merogony.

Amphidiploid as Species

The original F1 hybrids show no pairing. They show a reasonable percentage of diploid gametes. Experiments should have conditions that self-fertilization could occur. Fertility and vigor of the F2 should be at least comparable to those of the diploid species. Experiments producing Amphidiploids have been unsuccessful and could not withstand natural conditions. (Ref Walter E. Lammerts, Why Not Creation, page 257)

For the amphidiploid to qualify as a species, the original F1 hybrids should show no pairing. They should give diploid gametes. Self-Fertilization should occur. F2 fertility and vigor should be comparable to the diploid species.

Lennart Johnson, gave an account of chromosome pairing, the intergenic crosses of Oryzopsis, Indian Mountain Rice, Stipa and Spear grass. He demonstrated that the number of pairs is proportional to the number of chromosomes involved. (They had to be non-homologous associations of chromosomes).

C.J. Bishop on "Reviews in Genetics and Cytology 1. Plant Breeding 1963" stated

That there is failure of the older chromosome homology and pairing to hold up as practical plant breeding. He also stated that the multivalent chromosome association was a major factor to determine the fertility of the individual plant.

Research however, failed to reveal any consistent relationship between chromosome association and plant fertility. (Ref Walter E. Lammerts Why Not Creation, page 259)

Simon and Dollar on "Cytological Aspects of Speciation in Two North American Teleosts 1963".

Their account on the rainbow and cutthroat trout, indicates the trout with 60 chromosomes, was rather recently developed from the cutthroat trout having 64 by two centric chromosome fusions involving a centromere shift. This occurred during the last glacial period of the Pleistocene, since the species were not isolated until the continuity of the Snake River. (Ref Walter E. Lammerts Why Not Creation, page 260)

Harlan Lewis on "Catastrophic Selection as a Factor in Speciation 1962" commented;

That the reorganization of the species chromosome genomes make-up is a rapid process in which all the differences become consolidated within a few generations. He postulated that structural and quantitative changes in chromosomes accumulate as homozygotes one by one over a long period of time through random fixation or by selection of those with presumed slight selective advantage. Lewis suggests interspecific hybridization or a mutator gene.

Lewis' views were that most areas from the Great Flood became arid. His views did not show how translocations or inversions became established. (Ref Walter E. Lammerts Why Not Creation page 260)

Dobzhansky showed that translocations in homozygous conditions are inviable. Of the four translocations, with the second and third chromosome of D. Melanogaster, only one could be established in homozygous or true breeding conditions. T. Dobzhansky "Translocations Involving the Second and Fourth Chromosomes of D. Melagonaster 1931.

Dobzhanksy says "A minor but rather annoying difficulty for the biologist is the habit human paleontologists have for flattering their egos by naming each to find a new species, if not a new genus. This causes not only a needles cluttering of of the nomenclature but seriously misleading because treating as a species what is not a species beclouds some important issues".

"There is fair morphological evidence that there were two species of Australopithecus, but their synchronous existence has not been confirmed by the finds at the same level at one site. (Ref, Elwyn L. Simons 'Some Fantasies in the Study of Hominoid Phylogeny"

Ernst Mayr said 'Yet, in spite of all these advances numerous unsolved problems remain. Let me single out only four aspects of natural selection which raise doubt in my troubled mind. 1./ The selection of genes vs. the selection of genotypes. Too rapid a rate of simultaneous selection against too many genes might eliminate the entire population. 2./ Measure of fitness, It is crucial to find an objective yardstick."It is not a basic error of methodology to apply such a generalized technique as mathematics to a unique field of events such as organic evolution?" 3./ The population is a unit of selection. 4./ Reproduction success. Natural Selection may be defenceless against certain genes".

Sylvio Fiala "Letter" Science , vol. 135 p.975. , wrote "With all due recognition to the greatness of Darwin's achievement, we cannot remain blind to the fact that not a single step in the evolutionary mechanism has been clarified. Evolution means primarily an increase in content of information in the case of DNA, but natural selection means only the elimination of error in information or mutation.

Mendel

Gregor Mendel,in the Augustinian monastery of Breunn, Bruno Czechoslovakia. In 1857, Mendel began his experiments on inheritance, working with the numerous varieties of the garden pea which seedsman offered for sale. He carried out observations and experiments in the monastery garden for seven years. The choice of his material proved to be fortunate, and he was able to present his meetings of the Natural History Society of Bruenn in the spring of 1865.

,

Mendel found that when these hybrids were self-fertilized or crossed among themselves, two different plants were produced. Approximately 75% of plants showed dominant character, and the remaining 25% showed the recessive character. (Ref John Klotz, Genes Genesis and Evolution pages 267, 268)

He found that the characteristics of height, colour in the first and second generations were in accordance with simple mathematical proportions.

Ref to Gregor Mendel;

Of the plant life, offspring of a plant positive (dominant) and a negative (recessive), plant/animal takes after the dominant parent. In the second generation, the dominant one predominates, then the negative one appears. In the third generation both appear about equally in descendants. I.e., if a giant pea is crossed with a dwarf variety, the offspring are all tall. In the second generation, they both appear in the giant variety in the proportion of 3 to 1. In the third/fourth generation, they are on average equal in number, but when the dwarfs are self-fertilised, all the successive offspring are dwarfs. The same happened with rabbits, cats, rats and dogs. This law also applied to man and apes. Inferring that apes appear among men. Therefore men would turn to apes in the negative characters.

The following investigations confirmed these results, from the original P1 generation. The hybrid is called the F1 (first filial generation), and the progeny produced by crossing the hybrids among themselves or by self-fertilizing the hybrids make up the F2 (second filial generation). In every case where dominance is a complete ratio of offspring is approximately three to one. Where dominance is not complete, the ratio in the F2 is 1:2:1 (for example, one red, two pink, and one white).

Mendel observed the behaviour of two characteristics that were inherited independently. He crossed a pea plant having yellow round seeds, with one having wrinkled green seeds, he found that the all progeny were round, yellow seeded. Both round and yellow appeared to be the dominant factors. When these round yellow-seeded plants were self-fertilized, or when they were crossed among themselves, he found that instead of the two orfiginal combinations of characters he had four character combinations, two of which were new - round green and wrinkled yellow. In this case, the number of offspring appeared in a definite ratio. He found that the ratio was approximately 9:3:3:1. The results were 315 round, yellow; 108 round, green; 101 wrinkled, yellow; and 32 wrinkled, green. (Ref John Klotz, Genes Genesis and Evolution page 269).

In the F1 all of the progeny will show both dominants, if dominance in both cases is complete. In the F2 9/16 of the plants will show both dominants, 3/16 one dominant, 3/16 the other dominant, and 1/16 both recessives. If a green seeded plant were crossed with a wrinkled, yellow seeded plant, the progeny would be all round, yellow - seeded. If these were crossed among themselves the progeny would still be 9/16 round yellow, 3/16 round green, 3/16 wrinkled yellow, and 1/16 wrinkled green. (Ref John Klotz, Genes Genesis and Evolution page 269)

Supposed Extinct Forms

Dawn Redwood - Metasequoia Glyptostroboides, this was supposedly extinct for 20 million years. Though in 1944, chinese forester Tsang Wang found it growing in the Sichuan province.

Coelacanth fish, a living specimen found in South Africa in 1937. It was believed to be extinct 50 to 120 million years ago. Another specimen was found in 1952, and another in the Indian Ocean, Madagascar August 1953. Later another 7 specimens of Latermeria were found.

The earliest rocks are found in the Archeozoic. Plants and animals found in Proterozoic rocks.

Mendelism and Biometry

Mendel's experiments on plants and animals positive (dominant) and negative (recessive) take after the dominant parent. If a variety of pea is crossed with dwarf variety the offspring are all tall. The second generation the giant variety is proportioned to 3 to 1. The third/fourth generation are average equal in number. The same applies to cats, dogs, rabbits,, and humans, , humans would turn to apes in negative characters.

The Theory of the Gene

The genes have tiny structures found in the nucleus of every cell. They appear to be protein in nature. Size genes appear to range from a small virus to the size of a protein molecule.

No reliable estimate can be given as to the number of genes found in an organism. It is generally believed that there are about 2,000 to 2,500 in the lily plant, and 2000 to 13000 in Drosophila, with a probable number of 5000. It is believed that the number of genes in man is higher. Huxley estimates it to be from four to six times larger than the number found in Drosophila. Estimates have been from 5000 to 42000.

Chromosomes

The genes are believed to be arranged in a linear order on structures known as chromosomes. They appear as bodies as cells dividing. They are not found in resting cells. The chromosome material appears to be present but not organized into the definite bodies to be identified as chromosomes. In these chromosomes, material is identified not as definite bodies.

It is not possible to see genes under a microscope. For chromosomes, their number is characteristic for the species. There is a relationship between the number of chromosomes and the complexity of species.

The highest chromosome number is of a protozoan, single-celled radiolarian, that has 1600. The geometrid moth has 224.

Reduction of Chromosomes

The chromosome reduction can only occur if a loss of centromere, the fixed point where the spindle fibre attaches to the chromosome in cell division. The number of chromosomes is determined by the number of centromeres.

Addition of Chromosomes

Many evolutionists believe that evolution has been from the addition of chromosomes. Muller stated that the establishment of such repeats is the only effective means of gene increase in evolution except polyploidy.

Many of the 'lower forms' have higher chromosomes than the 'higher forms'. There is little or no evidence that evolution has occurred by adding one chromosome and then another second chromosome to the chromosome complex. Polysomics cannot occur from transverse fragmentation of chromosomes. This would result in additional centromeres.

Huxley said that while deficiency is not an uncommon occurrence in laboratory stocks of Drosophila, it is probably of little evolutionary significance in either in Drosophila or in other forms, because homozygous deficiencies are often lethal.

Some believe that gains/losses in genetic material could be established in the course of evolution unless they were very small. Deficiencies are usually semi-lethal/lethal when homozygous. (Ref G. Ledyard Stebbins "Variation and Evolution in Plants" 1950, page 189)

Homozygous Hemizygous

Hemizygous refers to when the condition of the male receives only a single "X" chromosome. A male carrying the "notch" would be on his "X" chromosome would be hemizygous for the "notch" (Ref John Klotz, Genes, Genesis and Evolution, page 327)

Dubinin Genetic Constitution and Gene Dynamics" reported the paracentric inversions of Drosophila. He found with Solokov and Tiviakov that eight paracentric inversions of 34,515 chromosomes in Drosophila. Paracentric do not include the centromere.

Stone and Griffin "Changing Structure of the Genome in Drosophila Melanogaster" 1940, pages 208-217,they were able to translocate the fourth chromosome to the "X" chromosome. Males became hemizygous. (Ref John Klotz, Genes Genesis and Evolution page 328)

Huxley believes that the gross morphology of the chromosomes throws littlelight on evolution. (Ref John Klotz, Genes Genesis and Evolution page 331)

Drosophila Melanogaster the haploid chromosome consists of two "V" s one rod, "X" chromosome, and the small fourth chromosome or microchromosome. D. Willistoni has no microchromosome. D. Virilis has five rods, and a microchromosome, D. Immigrants has one "V" and three rods. (Ref John Klotz, Genes, Genesis and Evolution page 331)

Homologous Chromosomes

Ordinarily these chromosomes are paired, and the two members of the pair are known as chromosomes. They contain the genes which have the same characteristics though the genes they bring about may not cause the same effect.

Sex Chromosomes and Sex Determination

Sex chromosomes these can be distinguished from other chromosomes, these are known as autosomes. In most animals one sex has a pair of sex chromosomes, and the other pair has only one of the sex chromosomes. Or it has a sex chromosome known as the "X" chromosome and a non-homologous, or only a partially homologous, "Y" chromosome. The "Y" chromosome is of a different size, shape. In some forms, as in man, the paired condition (homogametic or "XX") produces the female and the unpaired (heterogametic or "XX") condition the male. Fowl produces the opposite, the paired condition produces the male, the unpaired the female.

Autosomes in man are believed to contain male-determining genes, and the sex chromosomes female-determining genes. (Ref John Klotz, Genes Genesis and Evolution page 275).

If one sex chromosome (X chromosome) is received, the number of female-determining genes does not equal the number of the male-determining genes found on autosomes. Genes determining two different factors are located on the same chromosome, which Mendel predicted will not occur.

Haploidy or Monoploidy each chromosome is represented once instead of twice.

Polyploidy, each chromosome is represented more than twice.

Triploids chromosomes is three times,

Tetraploids chromosomes is four times

Octoploids chromosomes is eight times

Autopolyploidy a polyploid derived from a single diploid individual.

Allopolyploidy or amphiploid, a polyploid derived from a hybrid between two diploids

Monosomics are organisms that have lost one chromosome from one set.

Polysomics are organisms that have gained one or more chromosomes in a set

.

Trisomics gained one chromosome in one set.

Trisomics have gained two chromosomes in one set

Double Trisomics have gained one chromosome in two sets.

Haploidy

Haploidy occurs regularly in the alternation of generations in plants, where one generation reproduces asexually and is diploid and the next generation reproduces and is haploid. Haploid plants are smaller than their diploid relatives, and their cells have a volume and a half that of the diploid cells.

Polyploidy

There is no doubt that polyploidy and tetraploidy has been the means of producing what are ordinarily regarded as new species. They do not interbreed with their parent forms. They are fertile when they are bred among themselves.

Ernst Mayr of "Speciation and Systematics" 1949, page 285, he states, polyploidy is the only proved mechanism of instantaneous speciation in sexually producing organisms.

Stebbins reports that allopolyploid species have been synthesised in 40 or more species. In that 50 to 100 naturally occurring species have been analyzed to be autopolyploids.

Polyploid series occur in which different species in a genus have chromosome numbers, which appear to be multiples of the same number. Edward Dodson "A Textbook of Evolution" 1952, page 365 explains this.

"If another gamete which fertilizes or by which is fertilized is a normal haploid gamete, the zygote is triploid. If then it meets another diploid gamete, the zygote is a tetraploid. Polyploidy may also develop as a result of an irregular mitosis (ordinary cell division)."

The reduction of the fertility in triploids is due to the fact that gametes are viable that receive one or two complete sets of chromosomes. If the monoploid number of chromosomes is nine, the triploid will contain 27.

The adding or subtracting gene blocks has made the case of supermales and superfemales in Drosophila. The fruit fly has the presence of two "X" chromosomes that produce a female, and presence of one "X" and one "Y" chromosome produces a male. A triploid stock has in Drosophila produced in every chromosome a triplet.. Females produce two sets of autosomes and two sets "X" chromosomes. Males produce one set of autosomes and one set of "X" chromosome, and one "Y" chromosome. The table below shows the possible combinations of Drosophila

Type of Sperm	Type of Chromosomes	Ratio of Sex	Egg To Autosomes
2 X, 2 A	1 X, 1 A	1.0	Triploid Female
2 X, 2 A	1 Y, 1 A	0.67	Intersex
2 X, 1 A	1 X, 1 A	1.5	Superfemale
2 X, 1 A	1 Y, 1 X	1.0	Diploid Female
1 X, 2 A	1 X, 1 A	0.67	Intersex
1 X, 2 A	1 Y, 1 A	0.33	Superfemale
1 X, 1 A	1 X, 1 A	1.0	Diploid Female
1 X, 1 A	1 Y, 1 A	0.5	Diploid Male

Types of Polyploidy

It has been suggested there are four types of Polyploidy, the Autopolyploids, segmental allopolyploids, true or genomic allopolyploids, auto allopolyploids. The first two conditions will appear in triploid or tetraploid forms. The third are found in tetraploid that have a higher degree of the diploid number. The final one is found in the hexaploid or more. (Ref John Klotz, Genes, Genesis and Evolution 50n page 320)

Stebbins suggested the Amphiloid, where a polyploid has arisen after hybridization between two more species are separated.

Genes

The fundamental units inherited are genes. These are tiny structures found in the nucleus of every cell. In genes they may range in size that of a small virus to that of a medium or large size molecule. It is believed there are 2000 to 2500 in the lily plant. 2000 to 13000 Drosophila.

Julian Huxley on 'Evolution the Modern Synthesis' 1943 page 50. He estimated that it was 2000 to 13000 genes in Drosophila.

J.N. Spuhler 'The Number \of Genes in Man' 1948 page 279.

He estimated it was 20,000 to 42,000 in Drosophila

(Ref John Klotz, Genes, Genesis and Evolution page 271, 1955)

Speciation

Speciation is thought to occur either by **allopatric mechanisms,** this is when a population is split into two or more geographically divided subdivisions that organisms cannot bridge. A formation of a new ocean separating two land masses from a result of continental drift. Or by **Sympatric mechanisms,** occurring when two subpopulations have become reproductively isolated without the first becoming geographically isolated. (Ref Denis Alexander, Creation or Evolution, Do We Have to Choose? Page 113)

Inheritance of Variation

George Mendel, an Austrian monk, crossed strains of peas and found a statistical pattern governing the inheritance of such characteristics as tall vs. dwarf growth habit. Tall (TT) habit was dominant to dwarf (tt), that the first generation hybrids (Tt) were all tall. The dwarf habit of growth did not show up until the second filial generation or F2, where one fourth of the plants were dwarf in the habit (tt). Such traits are called recessive, and some are due to two factors so occur in only 1/16 of the F2 population n, and others due to three factors occurred in the 1/64 of the F2 plants.

Mendel, by a vast series of experiments in plant and animal life, has proved several natural laws of heredity. One of these is that the first offspring of a positive (Dominant) and a negative (Recessive) plant or animal takes after the dominant parent. In the second generation, the dominant one predominates, but the negative one appears. In the third or fourth generation both appear about equally in the descendants. E.g. if a giant variety of peas is crossed with a dwarf variety, the offspring are tall; in the second generation both appear, the giant variety proportion is 3 to 1.

(Ref Epiphany Studies In The Scriptures Series 2 Creation Paul S Johnson page 547, 1938)

Mutations

Mutations are sudden heritable changes in living species. The basic evolutionary argument is that favourable mutations give an advantage to natural selection.

1./ It is estimated that over 99% of mutations are harmful. 90% are lethal to the organisms that contain them.

2./ Macro-evolution requires not one but a multitude of simultaneous changes in an organism. None could survive unless there was a perfect coadaptation of it's new components developed.

3./Not all mutations are heritable. There is no evidence in the genetic code that will induce them always to continue in the same direction as they began.

4./Mutational Changes tend to be very slow.

Goldschmidt believed that mutations at most can bring about changes within species, and subspecies and varieties are formed, but not in incipient species. Richard Goldschmidt 'The Material Basis of Evolution' 1940 page 183

A good example of natural mutation is the Ancon sheep, a breed of sheep. In 1791, in a flock of Seth Wright, A New England farmer found a male lamb with short legs 15 ewes were heterozygous. When the Ancon ram was bred to these. Ancon offspring were produced. Of the 15 lambs produced two were of new type.

J.B.S. Haldane 'The Equilibrium Between Mutation and Random Extinction' 1939 , pages 400 to 405

Haldane explains;

'That if a mutation occurs with some favourable quality, the chances are strongly against its survival in the species'

It has been demonstrated that coefficients of .01 corresponding to the 1% advantage have been demonstrated.

The two types of changes that can occur to the sequence of the genes specifying functional proteins: **Neutral Mutations**, these have no effect on function and are substituted by drift; and are **advantageous mutations,** that have a positive effect on function and are substituted by selection.

J.W.Ewens "Comments on Dr. Kimura's Paper" Genetics said;

"I note the well known fact that the neutral theory predicts a constant rate of substitution per generation, whereas we appear to observe more a constant rate per year. In some of the species for which protein sequence comparisons have been made, there is a difference of one or even two orders of magnitude in generation time. It surely gets us nowhere simply to assume that the mutation rate adjusts itself in species of different generation time so that constant rates per year will arise"

(Ref Micheal Denton, Evolution, A Theory In Crisis, page 298, 1996)

Organism	Mutation Rate Per Nucleotide Per Year
E. Coli	0.7×10^6
Drosophila	2.5×10^8
Mouse	3.0×10^9
Man	1.0×10^{10}

Mutation Rates per time

Alan C. Wilson "Biochemical Evolution" page 611, 1977. Comments;

"The proteins that have evolved most slowly are supposed to have the highest proportion of sites at which functional constraints are particularly severe. According to this view, nearly every mutation that could occur in the gene for histone4*. Would be deleterious to the function of that histone."

The histones are a group of proteins which are associated with the DNA in all eukaryotes.

Mutations are a result of a "mistakes" in the process of gene reproduction, or the duplication of the deoxyribose nucleic acid or DNA molecules which either are or house genes which determine the characteristics of plants and animals. Cosmic radiation, chemical mutagens cause mutations.

Some mutations are advantageous. Bacteria when exposed to high levels of penicillin, or streptomycin, most die out. Sometimes one may live to a mutation tolerance of these antibiotics. There is also mutation by segregation by the already existing variability - heterozygosity, that occurs then stops.

Careful intercrosses and back-crosses showed that these mutations could be grouped into four linkage groups corresponding to the four chromosomes of species. Within each chromosome the mutant genes were located serially. The order of their sequence was determined by crossing-over studies. Chromosome mapping can be done, though there can be the odd clumping of genes. (Ref Walter E. Lammerts Why Not Creation page 299).

The process of mutation was greatly speeded up by X-Ray irradiation of the fruit fly. Experiments by Muller in 1928 and by Morgan. It was disappointing, that for evolution-minded biologists most mutations were harmful. One in a thousand seemed to be neutral or showed slight advantage under laboratory methods of nutrient agar culture. X-rays did not prove to be effective for variations in plants. Most mutations were of semi-sterile types to be a result of translocations. Portions of the chromosomes formerly separate were attached, and reciprocally. Haldane, Fischer, Sewell Wright stated that one in a thousand mutations was an advantage of one percent, these would accumulate under natural selection then lead to evolutionary change.

H.T. In "Natural Selection and Concealed Genetic Variability in a Natural Population of Melongaster" she concentrated on the populations of melanogaster the fruit flew between 1947 and 1962. She stated that natural selection does not increase the most viable or the best true breeding lines or homozygotes in natural populations.

It is evident that there is no evidence of selection which has been primarily directed to the elimination of harmful variations or mutations. The variants do not reduce the viability of the heterozygote. Her research showed that most viable homozygotes do not increase in number, and no viability occurs. The ratio of the "harmful" to "useful" is around 1,000 to 1 in mutations. If a species did evolve by natural selection, the genetic load of a drastic or harmful mutation would be so high, that in a few hundred generations as a result all offspring having some defect, because of chance mating of identical genotypes resulting in homozygosity. (Ref Walter E. Lammerts Why Not Creation page 303).

Mutations, it is now understoods are not superior. The germ tissue, and the organization of the molecules within the cells are sufficiently delicate and precise that any disruption, such as a damage to a gene or shearing of a chromosome, is almost sure to be in the direction of disorganization and balance, to say inferior (Ref Donald Patten, Biblical Flood, Ice Epoch page 239). It is further known that mutations are recessive than dominant. They are not expressed as a pair with a normal gene, the dominant one.

Darwin thought changes to interbreeding would be sometimes superior, sometimes inferior. And equal in ratios. This has not been the case. They are sometimes adaptive,and are more likely to be neutral/inferior in a proportion greater than 99% of the time. Mutations are deranged genes and that they may be inherited generation after generation. When inbreeding occurs, defective mutations are matched in higher increasing proportions, closer the relationship of the parents become.

Darwin's views were unscientific, lack of knowledge etc,. Hugh Iltis made the following comments;

"The basic notion of Darwin's doctrine was the variability of the species whereas the basic idea of Mendel's (though none of Mendel's hearers or even the lecturer himself had clearly recognised this) was the constancy if not of the species, at least of their elements or characters, and the heredity factors producing these........The trouble was this, and this only, that the time was not yet ripe for the understanding of Mendel's law either in Brunn or elsewhere" (Ref Donald Patten Biblical Flood, Ice Epoch page 240).

Advantageous Mutations; spreading to all members of species;

Substitution rate depends on;

1./Mutation Rate

2./Generation Time

3./Total Population Number

Teilhard de Chardin wrote;

'A mutation therefore as fundamental as that though, a mutation which gives it's specific impetus to the whole human group could not in my opinion have appeared half-way up the stalk. It dominates the whole edifice, it's place must therefore be beneath every recognizable vertical in the unattainable depths and this beneath those sea creatures which (however pre-hominid in cranial structures) are already situated above the point of origin and blossoming of the race'

Theodosius Dobzhansky said this on mutations;

'The process of mutation is the only known source of the new materials of genetic variability and hence of evolution.....An apparent paradox has been disclosed. Although the matter becomes adapted to its environment through formation of superior genetic patterns from mutational components, the **process of mutations itself is not adaptive.** On the contrary, the mutations which arise are, with rare exceptions, **deleterious to their carriers.** At least in the environments, which species normally encounters. **Some of them are deleterious apparently in all environments.** Therefore, the mutation process alone, not corrected and guided by natural selection would result in **degeneration and extinction rather than improved adaptiveness.'**

Dobzhanksy explains how change mutation is affected by micro and macro evolution;

'The Gene change in mutation, and gene frequency, change by natural selection'.

Are the most important common denominators in both micro and macro-evolution.'

(Ref Theodosius Dobzhansky 'On The Methods of Evolutionary Biology and Anthropology, 1957, page 385)

Dobzhanksy said this in Principles of Genetics 1950, page 315;

'Since mutation is the only known method of origin of new hereditary variability,

The mutation process is considered to be the prime source of the materials of evolution' ;

Ernst Hooton, an anthropologist said this,

'Saltatory evolution by way of mutation, is a very convenient way of bridging over gaps **between animal forms**. Now, I am afraid that many anthropologists, including myself, have sinned against genetic science and are leaning upon a broken reed'.
(Ref Ernst A Hooton, Apes, Men and Morons, 1937 page 118)

Parallel Mutations

A well known phenomena of parallel mutations, the fruit flies Drosophila melanogaster and D. Simulans are two separate species, they both have experienced mutations of eye colour to prune, ruby, and garnet; of body colour to yellow; of bristle shapes to forked to bobbed; of wings to crossveinless vesiculated, and rudimentary.

Another example would be albinism, which appears as a mutation in a great many animal forms, and also in many plants. In some cases it is probably a parallel mutation, but in many cases different genes are involved. These are frequently known as mimic genes.

De Vries and the Mutation Theory

De Vries worked on the evening primrose at the Oenothera Lamarckiana. He found it in an abandoned potato field. Specimens were transferred to his garden, and due to his experiments he noticed a number of abrupt changes that he called "mutations". .De Vries called them a new species.

These new species were really varieties. De Vries 'Mutations' were not mutations, they were due the breeding out of the recessive characters present in the stock but not showing themselves (similar to the birth of an albino child to normal parents who are carriers.
(Ref John Klotz, Genes, Genesis and Evolution, pages 38-40)

One biologist had suggested "A species is a group of individuals which, in the sum total of their attributes, resemble each other to a degree usually accepted as specific, the exact degree being ultimately determined by the more or less arbitrary judgement of taxonomists". (Ref J.S.L. Gilmour "Taxonomy and Philosophy" page 468, 1940)

We are told that "a species is a community or a number of related communities, whose distinctive morphological characters (those concerned with the form and structure of the organism) are, in the opinion of a competent systematist, sufficiently definite to entitle them to a new specific name. (Ref C. Tate Began, "Organic Evolution" 1925, 1926)

Huxley believed that species are natural units which meet four criteria,

1./ They have a definite geographical range.

2./ They are self-perpetuating groups

3./ They are distinguishable in form and external appearance from other related groups, or in rare cases where they are externally similar they may be distinguished by apparent chemical differences in the structure of protoplasm.

4./They do not normally interbreed with related groups, in most cases showing partial or total infertility on crossing with them.

(Ref John Klotz Genes, Genesis and Evolution page 47)

Mayr believed that species are groups of actually or potentially interbreeding populations that are reproductively isolated from other such groups.
(Ref Ernst Mayr, "Speciation and Systematics". Genetics Paleontology and Evolution 1949, page 284)

G. Ledyard Stebbins, Variation and Evolution in Plants 1950, page 189, he commented "In sexually reproducing organisms, a species is a system consisting of one or more genetically, morphologically, and physiologically different kinds of organisms which possess an essential continuity maintained by the similarity of genes between its members. Species are separated from each other by gaps of genetic discontinuity in morphological and physiological characteristics, which are maintained by the absence or rarity of gene interchange between members of different species."

A.H. Sturtevant The Classification of the Genus Drosophila with Descriptions of Nine New Species, 1942, page 32, stated these three criteria for species;

1./ Species must be separable on the basis of ordinary material.

2./Cross fertility between distinct species are generally absent or so slight as to make an unlikely transfer of genes from one to another in nature.

3./ Subspecies usually replace one another geographically. Species may do so, but are more likely to show extensively overlapping distributing areas.

(Ref John Klotz, Genes, Genesis and Evolution page 48)

Stebbins made this statement "As our knowledge of the biological facts becomes more complete, we shall gradually achieve a firmer basis, consisting of a large fund of common knowledge on which to erect our species concept"

Existence of Species / Mutations

Two oaks, Quercus robur and Q. sessiliflora are kept separate not only by the fact that the first grows on lime soil, but the second does not. Red grouse (Lagopus scoticus) Britain, Willow grouse (L. lagopus) Scandinavia. Two separate species, when either is introduced in the geographical range of each other aliens interbreed.

Linneaus believed that there were two species of peas, Pisum arvense and P. sativum. Biologists believe that these are single species. When they are crossed they form a fertile hybrid. (Ref John klotz Genes, Genesis and Evolution pages 52 to 53)

Huxley said "Experience has taught that in some cases large differences in appearance are possible within an interbreeding group. The colour phases of some birds mammals are examples, but the most striking cases are those of polymorphic mimicry in butterflies. The older entomologists were shocked at the idea that such diverse types might belong to the same species".

Huxley states deer mice are marked inter sterility and appear with a small degree of morphological difference.
(Ref John Klotz Genes, Genesis and Evolution page 54)

There have been nineteen forms of spotted hyena (Crocuta crocuta). Taxonomists regard this as belonging to one species. It is believed to be no more than three subspecies.

George Gaylord Simpson "Rates of Evolution in Animals" 1949, he commented, that subspecies and local races may evolve in less than a century, but commonly require 10,000 years or so. Species require 50,000 years at least for evolution.

Mayr believes that the evolution of species requires a minimum of several hundred thousand years and averages a million years or more. Speciation requires a time interval equivalent of roughly to 30,000 human generations. Ernst Mayr "Speciation and Selection" 1949 (Ref John Klotz, Genes, Genesis and Evolution page 115).

Huxley said that in forms such as the horse the time needed to effect the change of specific magnitude is in the order of 100,000 generations and of generic magnitude, of a million generations.

Agamic Complex

Agamic complexes are referred to forms with hybridization, polyploidy, and apomixis, an example of this is the hawk's beard, Crepis. Crepis is made up of a number of polyploids in which the basic haploid chromosome number is 11. There are a few genuses which are sexual diploids, they only constitute only a minute fraction. The polyploids show chromosome numbers 33, 44, 55, 77, and 88. (Ref John Klotz, genes, Genesis and Evolution page 63). It has been shown that the polyploid characteristics found in the diploid species and the polyploidy does not occur as would be expected in evolution.

Huxley also mentions hybrid swarms are presumably formed by introgressive hybridization. Over a short period of time agamic complexes and similar forms are believed to be capable of a rapid burst of evolution. Agamic complexes consist mainly of apomicts. There is no evidence that apomicts evolved to a genus or sub-genus.

Mayr says that no system of nomenclature and no hierarchy of systematic categories is able to represent adequately nature as it actually is. (Ref John Klotz, Genes, Genesis and Evolution page 65)

Hybridization

The definition is described as crosses between different types of species. Assuming 10,000 loci in the monoploid number of man, and if there are two alleles at each locus, the number of possible genotypes for the human population would be approx 3 to the power 10,000. No human beings will have the same background.

(Ref C.D. Darlington "The Evolution of Genetic Systems" 1939, page 77) He calculated a recombination index, this was determined by the chromosome number, the number of chiasmata, breaks in the chromosome which determines the amount of crossing over. Hybridization does not produce new species. It can produce sub-species within a species. (Ref Ernst Mayr "Systematics and the Origin of Species" 1942, page 270), believed that hybridization, instead of promoting speciation accomplishes the opposite. He believes that it eliminates the gap between two populations or two sub-species. (Ref John Klotz, Genes, Genesis and Evolution page 395).

Ernst Mayr 'Systematics and the Original Species' 1942 page 270.

Heterozygosity, an example of this would be Oenothera, (Evening Primrose) These plants are almost permanent hybrids/permanent heterozygotes. Each of these species contains two gene complexes and at meiosis, each separates each other as a single entity.
(Ref John Klotz, Genes, Genesis and Evolution page 398).

Introgressive Hybridization, this involves the introduction of genes from one species by crossing of the two species and a back crossing of the parents.

Recombination Is limited, the reduction division (process in which the chromosome number is reduced to the haploid number, the chromosomes from the parents pair and exchange genes. The genes are shuffled so that the offspring do not inherit a solid block of genes from one parent.

Vascular plants already existed in the Silurian period. The Bryophytes were unknown fossils until the Pennsylvanian period. Most evolutionists believe that the bryophytes are a terminal group and did not give rise to higher forms. (Ref John Klotz, Genes, Genesis and Evolution page 432)

Plants appeared greatly in the late Cretaceous period. It is assumed that they must of originated earlier, not because of fossils, but it is inconceivable that they originated suddenly. (Ref John Klotz, Genes, Genesis and Evolution page 433)

Introgressive Hybridization

This involves the introduction of genes from one species into the gene complex to another species by crossing of the two species and then a backcrossing to one of the parents. Polyploidy is often associated with Hybridization. Hybridization is more important in plants than animals. (Ref M.J.D. White "Animal Cytology and Evolution" 1948, page 217)

Heterozygosity

In most species each plant produces two types of gametes, differing not in a single gene, but in very many closely linked genes. The set of genes carried in a given complex is constant and held together through the life cycle. Each of the species Oenothera, according to this hypothesis contains two of these genes, or gene complexes, and at meiosis each separates from the other as a single entity.
(Ref John Klotz, Genes, Genesis and Evolution pages 398-399)

Quantum Evolution

This is an explosive type of evolution where a shifting of a new type of adaptation occurs. The first being an adaptive phase where the group loses it's the equilibrium of its ancestors/collaterals. In this phase organisms lose their fitness and have a poor adaptation to the environment.

The second phase is the preadaptive phase, where there is a great selective pressure to move a group to a new equilibrium.

The adaptive phase is the third stage of quantum evolution. This where the organism reaches a new equilibrium with its environment. It develops stability before undergoing this quantum evolution. (Ref E.B Ford "Mendelism and Evolution" 1949 page 78)

Sewall Wright, Genetic Drift

It is believed that non-useful characters have appeared in species, and in a small population, a large number of the organisms will be eliminated by random causes rather than by selection.

The problem with this is that this would only account for a non useful character in a small population with a high mutation rate. There have been many non-useful characters in populations that have been large, but not a high mutation rate. (Ref Sewall Wright "The Statistical Consequence of Mendelian Heredity in Relation to Speciation" 1940, page 164). Sewall Wright believes that the process of evolution is the change in the gene frequency and not the mutation itself. (Ref John klotz, genes, Genesis and Evolution pages 403-405)

Ford has the opinion that the genetic drift has of little importance to evolution. He believes the evidence indicates that there is no significance in evolution where the population is 1,000 individuals or more.

Parallelism

Parallelism is a type of evolution where two species are evolving on a parallel line. These have diverged from a common ancestor, but have continued to develop along a parallel line. Drosophila Melanogaster and D. Simulans, are believed to be examples of parallel evolution.

Drosophila

From one or two original colonizations by the fruit fly Drosophila, like 600 to 700 unique Hawaiin species had evolved. The study of Drosophila in Hawaii, had revealed one of the most dramatic cases where "perfect" sequential arrangements have provided compelling evidence that new species do arise from pre-existing species. (Ref Micheal Denton, Evolution, A Theory in Crisis, page 82, 1996)

By studying the order of genes along the chromosomes in the various Drosophila species on the different islands have found a number of perfect evolutionary sequences and have been able to work out the entire evolutionary history of most of the Hawaiian species. (Ref Micheal Denton, Evolution, A Theory in Crisis, page 82, 1996)

A universal view is that the geographical isolation of a population is the key event to the road of species formation. (This account was given by Ernst Mayr "Animal Species and Evolution, page 84, 1996)

Geographical isolation prevents interbreeding with the parent population and allows the isolated daughter population to undergo unique adaptive changes leading eventually to the formation of distinct subspecies. Later, when the newly evolved sub-species with its unique characteristics comes into contact with it's parent species. Hybrids are a selective disadvantage and isolating mechanisms evolve to prevent interbreeding. Eventually, full reproductive isolation evolves, converting sub-species into a new species.

Plant species have been formed suddenly by massive chromosomal mutations which create instantly a new daughter population reproductively isolated from it's parental stock.
(Ref Micheal Denton, Evolution, A Theory in Crisis, page 85, 1996)

Linkage and crossing-over in Drosophila (Involving a cross of a normal fly with a grey coloured body and wings with a black-bodied and vestigial winged fly)

Convergence

The wolf and the Tasmanian wolf are believed to be examples of convergence (Thylacinus cynocephalus)

Convergence is meant that by the development of similar characteristics in two forms which had radically different ancestors.

Huxley in his "Evolution the Modern Synthesis" refers to different modes of speciation; successional, divergent, convergent, reticulate.

Successional Speciation, groups have been isolated by time. One species has given rise to another species. The new species separate gradually. Morphological differences develop gradually. Being separated by time,, they cannot interbreed.

Divergent Speciation; Huxley believes there are eight kinds of evolution. One species has gradually divided into two or more species. In thres of these four types of divergent evolution the isolation is a spatial one, and in the fifth it is isolation as genetic.
(Ref John Klotz, Genes, Genesis and Evolution, pages 411 to 412)

Hybridization

The definition is described as crosses between different types of species. Assuming 10,000 loci in the monoploid number of man, and if there are two alleles at each locus, the number of possible genotypes for the human population would be approx 3 to the power 10,000. No human beings will have the same background.

(Ref C.D. Darlington "The Evolution of Genetic Systems" 1939, page 77) He calculated a recombination index, this was determined by the chromosome number, the number of chiasmata, breaks in the chromosome which determines the amount of crossing over. Hybridization does not produce new species. It can produce sub-species within a species. (Ref Ernst Mayr "Systematics and the Origin of Species" 1942, page 270), believed that hybridization, instead of promoting speciation accomplishes the opposite. He believes that it eliminates the gap between two populations or two sub-species. (Ref John Klotz, Genes, Genesis and Evolution page 395)

Recombination Is limited, the reduction division (process in which the chromosome number is reduced to the haploid number, the chromosomes from the parents pair and exchange genes. The genes are shuffled so that the offspring do not inherit a solid block of genes from one parent.

Vascular plants already existed in the Silurian period. The Bryophytes were unknown fossils until the Pennsylvanian period. Most evolutionists believe that the bryophytes are a terminal group and did not give rise to higher forms. (Ref John Klotz, Genes, Genesis and Evolution page 432)

Plants appeared greatly in the late Cretaceous period. It is assumed that they must of originated earlier, not because of fossils, but it is inconceivable that they originated suddenly. (Ref John Klotz, Genes, Genesis and Evolution page 433)

Protozoa

Protozoa are simple one-celled organisms. These could not have existed without plants. Euglena was believed to be the link to plants and animals. The first of the true protozoa is believed to have a form similar to modern heliozoa or radiolaria.

Heliozoa are one-celled organisms surrounded by a gelatinous matrix - lattice like case. They have many radiating strands of protoplasm known as pseudopods "sun animalcules". They mainly live in freshwater. The radiolaria are similar to heliozoa. Their cytostome is separated into an inner and outer portion of the capsule. They have a skeleton of silica/strontium sulfate. They are marine and pelagic, living in the ocean. (Ref John Klotz, Genes, Genesis and Evolution page 436)

There have been reports of radiolaria in preCambrian rock. There is no real evidence they exist in Proterozoic and Archeozoic rocks. Cambrian rocks, the protozoa make up 0.4% of the fauna. Amoeba are only known from the late Paleozoic rocks of the Carboniferous period. (Ref John Klotz, Genes, Genesis and Evolution pages 437-438.)

Sponge Evolution

Sponges have developed from a specialized type of protozoa called Choanoflagellate. These are flagellates that belong to the Euglena. Each of the single-celled individuals has a long lash, or flagellum surrounded by a funnel or delicate protoplasmic collar. Sponges are the main line for evolution.

Arthropods

The arthropods are regarded as the highest form of the invertebrates. Mollusks are in its equal. The earliest of the arthropods are the trilobites. They are found in the lower Cambrian rocks. They are sometimes known as "rock bugs". Each of their body segments have a pair of undifferentiated appendages. They are believed to be parapods of the annelids, but were joined. Their head was covered with a dorsal shield.

Some evolutionists believe that the trilobites were ancestral to modern crustaceans. Most evolutionists believe that trilobites and crustaceans are parallel offshoots of a primitive pre-Cambrian annelid.

The mollusks are regarded as a peculiar branch of this stock. Trilobites, and other arthropods are regarded as progressive descendants of this stock. Mollusks developed a skeleton of lime. Trilobites then developed a skeleton of chitin.

It is believed Trilobites then gave rise to forms to primitive horse-shoe crabs, and scorpions. Crustaceans cast off their old skin as their bodies increase in size. Mollusks cannot do this. (Ref John Klotz, Genes Genesis and Evolution, pages 447-448)

Origin of Insects

It was thought that trilobites gave rise to insects. Many evolutionists believe that insects developed directly from the preCambrian annelid stock. De-Beer suggests they originated from the larvae of some myriapod forms of a retention of juvenile characters. (Ref Genes Genesis Evolution John Klotz, 155)

Eclectic Theory, Gregory says characteristics found in various invertebrate forms are eclectic. These features are not found in any single invertebrate form, but in several invertebrate forms

Problems with Vertebrate Origins

The invertebrates, annelids and arthropods, have a ventral nerve cord. Their nerve cord is solid, their hearts are dorsal. The vertebrates have a dorsal nerve cord, their hearts are ventral. (Ref Genes Genesis Evolution John Klotz, 155)

The vertebrates did not appear till the time of the highest Silurian beds (Ludlow), in which was found the oldest known fish, the Pteraspis.

Agassiz, classified fishes by the following;

1./ The Placoids, (From broad plate), having an internal cartilaginous skeleton,

were covered externally with armature plates, and points of bone.

2./ The Ganoids, (From Splendour) referring to the brilliant surface of their enamels, armour of enamelled bone, bony plates that lock into each other at their edges, like Sturgeon.

3./ The Ctenoid, (From a comb) Fishes covered with scales that of a horny substance and pectinated at the lower edges, like teeth of a comb, as in Perch.

4./ The Cycloids (From a circle) whose scales are like a continuous margin, like Salmon.

(Ref Samuel Kinns PH.D.,F.R.A.S. The Harmony of the Bible and Science, pages 263, 264, 1895)

Cytochrome

No animal cytochrome is an intermediate between animals and the other 2 eucaryote groups.

Cytochrome C varied less between species than haemoglobin;

The haemoglobin sequences of man and dog differed by 20%, but the Cytochrome sequences varied by 5%.

The haemoglobin sequences of man and carp varied by 50%, but the Cytochrome sequences varied by 13%.

(Ref Micheal Denton, Evolution, A Theory in Crisis, page 276, 1996)

All cytochrome C molecules are about one hundred amino acids long. A taxonomic distance increases, example between a horse and a dog (two mammals) the divergence is 6%, between a horse and a turtle (two vertebrates) the divergence is 11%., between the horse and fruit fly (two animals) the divergence is 22%. (Ref Micheal Denton, Evolution, A Theory In Crisis, page 278, 1996).

There are no intermediates to bridge the gap between procaryotes and eucaryotes.

(Ref Micheal Denton, Evolution, A theory in crisis, page 281, 1996)

Haemoglobin differs by 50% between man and carp, the cytochrome C differs by 13%.

The Haemoglobin sequences of a particular group differ from 50%, all cytochrome C sequences differ about 13%. It is necessary for evolutionary theory to presume that the molecular clock has ticked a faster rate in haemoglobin than in the case of cytochrome C.

The two types of changes that can occur to the sequence of the genes specifying functional proteins: **Neutral Mutations**, these have no effect on function and are substituted by drift; and are **advantageous mutations,** that have a positive effect on function and are substituted by selection.

J.W.Ewens "Comments on Dr. Kimura's Paper" Genetics said;

"I note the well known fact that the neutral theory predicts a constant rate of substitution per generation, whereas we appear to observe more a constant rate per year. In some of the species for which protein sequence comparisons have been made, there is a difference of one or even two orders of magnitude in generation time. It surely gets us nowhere simply to assume that the mutation rate adjusts itself in species of different generation time so that constant rates per year will arise"

(Ref Micheal Denton, Evolution, A Theory In Crisis, page 298, 1996)

Life Germ

Evolutionists guess that the earth being 16,000,000 to 8,000,000,000 years so that the earth would cool off so that evolution would work from the first life germ for sufficient time to produce 3,000,000 species. Some scientists have claimed the earth to be 18,000,000 years. It was from gases thrown off from our universal spiral that the sun and the solar system was formed. Scientist Helmholtz stated light and heat are caused by its contracting. Helmholtz, Kelvin, Young, Todd have 'demonstrated' that this contraction causing a shrinking of about 300 ft annually in the sun's diameter, would be sufficient to keep up the light and heat at their present quantity. Prof Young in astronomy said' The shrinkage of the sun to its present dimensions from a diameter larger than the orbit of Neptune, the remotest of the planets would generate about 18,000,000 times as much heat as the sun radiates in a year. If the sun's heat and still is due to the contraction of its mass, it cannot have been radiating heat at the present rate, on the shrinking hypothesis for more than 18,000,000 years. It proves that even 18,000,000 years, the gas that was developed into the earth and its sun left it's common spiral.

Millions of years were required before the molten mass that formed the earth cooled off enough to form an adequate crust to permit animal and plant life to live upon, this disproves evolution. Lord Kelvin calculated that the sun's age was at 18,000,000 years, and calculated the earth's age at 8,302,210 years. If we subtract the years the time necessary for the earth to cool off sufficiently and to form a thick crust to sustain animal and plant life, there would be not enough time for the evolution of 3,000,000 species, for several million years must of lapsed in the cooling process and in the formation of a crust averages 25 miles deep over the fiery mass within the earth.

If plants evolved from an original germ, how did it get distributed in continents separated by oceans, before man appeared on the earth? The change of species, and its process from its change from one to another, animal fossil changing, surely there must have been evidence in the earth's strata to indicate this, there isn't. Agassiz, one of the leading scientists said on evolution 'is a scientific mistake, untrue in it's facts, unscientific in its methods and mischievous in it's tendencies.'

Dawn Redwood - Metasequoia glyptostroboides. This was supposedly extinct for 20 million years. However, in 1944 Chinese forester Tsang Wang found it growing in Sichuan province. Specimens of Dawn Redwood supposedly were from the late cretaceous period 90 million years ago, then went into the Cenozoic period 65 million years ago.

Jerry Coyne wrote this about multicell-organisms;

'About 600 million years ago, a whole gamut of relatively simple but multicell- organisms arose. Including worms jellyfish and sponges. These groups diversified over the next several million years, with terrestrial plants and tetrapods and four-legged animals, first being the lobe finned fish, which appeared 400 million years ago'.

This account from Coyne raises questions, He gives an account of 600 million and 400 million years, but nothing of the 540 million year Cambrian Explosion event.

Empedocles (493-435BC) believed that plants and animals were not produced simultaneously. Plants he thought, originated first, and animal life came into existence only much later. He also suggested a sort of "survival of the fittest". Aristotle (384-322BC) believed in a complete gradation of nature. He believed that there had been a gradual transition from the imperfect to the perfect, and that man stood the highest.

Francis Bacon 1561 - 1626, called the attention to the variations in animals and the bearing of this variation upon the origin of new species. Leibnitz (1656 - 1716) believed that all the different classes of animals were connected by transitional forms. Kant (1724 -1804) believed that higher organisms developed from simpler forms.

Buffon (1707 - 1788) French naturalist, biologist to theory of evolution suggested the concept for the struggle for existence.

Carolus Linneaus (1707 - 1778) set up the present classification system, a believer in the absolute fixity of species.

Jean Baptiste Lamarck (1744 - 1829) suggested a near complete theory of evolution and in greater detail in the Philosophie Zoologique.

He developed his theory in the following four postulates;

1./ Life by it's own efforts tends continually to increase the volume of everything which it posses and to increase the size of it's parts up to a limit which life itself determines.

2./The formation of a new organ is the result of a new need which has arisen and continues to be felt by the organism.

3./The extent of development of organs and their power of action is proportional to their use.

4/ All changes occuring during the lifetime of an organism are transmitted to its offspring by the process of reproduction.

(Ref John Klotz, Genes, Genesis and Evolution pages 23 -24)

The term 'Tohu va bohu' The earth was void and formless, as in Jeremiah 4:23. By this account, it has been seriously considered by geologists that the millions of years old actually took place so that it would make fossils possible.Though, understanding scripture Genesis 1:2, says that the world was not disorganized. The hebrew interpretation is unorganized. The understanding of 'void and formless' is that the world was waste and empty, barren. It does not mean laying waste, empty. In conclusion, it could really be said that it was formless, lifeless. The following hebrew terms are used. Bara, asah, yatsar.

(Ref Genes Genesis and Evolution, John Klotz. Page 92, 1955)

Bara is referring to 'ex-nihilo' that is created from nothing 'zero' Asar, Yatsar would refer to creating, but from something already in existence. Gen 1:1 bara is used. It is also used in Gen 1:21 and in 1:27.

Genesis 1:26 asah is used for Moses

Genesis 2:7, yatsar is used. And we can then say, in Gen 1:31 'The lord saw everything it was very good', having understood this, it could not account for evil angels that had destroyed some of the world.

(Ref Genes Genesis and Evolution, John Klotz. Page 95, 1955)

It can be said that the world was left populated, Genesis 1:28, 9:1, and it is shown that from Gen 5 to Gen 11, how the spread of the human race was, ages included the large number of sons and daughters the world was populated quickly. This would indicate the world was not billions of years.

Chapter 6

Trilobites

Trilobites were arthropods, with soft parts of their bodies covered with an exoskeleton, and the dorsal with exoskeleton. The word 'Trilobite' refers to the three lobes. It has been suggested there are 20,000 plus species of Trilobites. The three parts the head (cephalon) the body (thorax) and the pygidium (tail).

The Trilobites were the extinct subphylum of the Anthropoda.

The largest Trilobite being the Isotelus Rex 720mm

                        Uralichus Hispanicus 680mm

                        Terataspis Grandis 600mm

                        Acadoparadoxides Briareus 450mm

                        Isotelus Brachycephalus 330mm

The examination of the eyes of a trilobite, which must have a nerve attached to it, and those nerves must have passed all into the brain. As early as Earth's history, as the Cambrian strata, animal life existed without a nervous system. Their eyes were composed and made up of calcite lenses.

Trilobites were benthic, and lived in shallow water. The Redlichidda was one of the oldest forms of Trilobites. It is believed that some species had up to 15,000 lenses in one eye.

How could such an animal with a perfect nervous system exist in the earliest and lower strata with none of the infinite gradations existing which evolution is required to produce ? Darwinists insisted that the gradations existed in the previous Huronian and Lauretian rocks.

Mr Etheridge in 1881, Geological Society said, from the Lower Cambrian of South Wales, Trilobites, Brachiopods,and others, "I particularly mention this first assemblage of life, as being as far as I know, the Earliest in the Earth's history, it consists of forms whose organisation was not embryonic."

(Ref Samuel D. Kinns PH. D., F.R.A.S. The Harmony of the Bible and Science, pages 260, 261, 1895)

Cave fish

Their development is based on an explanation of so-called "loss mutations". This loss would cause the extinction of the individual, as he would be unable to compete. It is suggested that these fishes swam into caves, their vision became useless, and eventually deteriorated.

It is suggested why these fish should swim in the darkness of caves. The reason is they originally came from forms that shunned light, living in corners and holes. It is believed that these light-shunning fish were no more likely to enter caves and it was easy for them to lose their visual powers through the occurrence of a few "loss mutations".

Huxley points out that 'Anoptichthys Jordani' is a blind fish found in caves of Mexico. With large eyes it's unlikely that it would wander in a cave by accident. (Ref Genes Genesis Evolution John Klotz, 1955)

The Choanata

Originally to have had paired lungs. The descendants, the Dipnoans, kept their paired lungs. The Crossopterygians have lost their paired lungs.

Lungfish at one time were very numerous, the first was the 'Dipterus' it appeared in the Devonian period. There were three genera and five species of lungfish, one in South America, one in Australia, and in Central Africa. (Ref Genes Genesis Evolution John Klotz, 1955)

The Coelenterate Theory

The Amphioxus, the supposed primitive pre-vertebrate. It was derived from a coelenterate, like Hydra or Jellyfish. The Amphioxus is a tiny fishlike organism lacking backbone or vertebral column. It contains a notochord, a rod of cells giving support to the animal. Many evolutionists consider the Amphioxus as a primitive chordate. This animal has no heart, blood is pumped by rhythmic contractions of the ventral aorta. (Ref john Klotz)

Phylum Coelenterata are invertebrate animals that are mainly attached to rocks at the bottom of the ocean. They have two layers of cells, the outer one is the ectoderm and the inner one the endoderm. Being diploblastic, they do not have sensory organs. Their bones/skeleton are calcium carbonate. Jellyfish and corals.

The coelenterate are solitary hydra or colonial obelia. Their bodies are circular cylindrical like. Their digestion is intracellular and extracellular, Their movement is by their tentacles and muscle fibres.

It is hard to believe that the vertebrates are derived from all of the invertebrates that have taken characteristics from each of the groups. Many of the tissues and structures are not homologous. And show only general analogies to vertebrate types. This would not fit the evolution theory of phylogenetic trees. (Ref Genes Genesis Evolution John Klotz, 1955)

Coelacanths

It was in 1938, fisherman in the Indian Ocean, off Cape Province, South Africa, hauled to the service a living relative of the ancient Rhipidistia - the Coelacanth.

Peter Forey "Latimeria: A Paradoxical Fish, page 369, 1996," commented on it's discovery;

"We had to wait nearly one hundred years before the discovery of the recent Coelacanth during that time many fossil coelacanths were described and, on the basis of osteological features, their systematic position as near relatives of the extinct rhipidistians and as tetrapod cousins had become a part of 'evolutionary fact', perpetuated today in textbooks........Here at last was a chance to glimpse the workings of a tetrapod ancestor. These expectations were founded on two premises. First, that Rhipidistians are the nearest relatives of tetrapods, and secondly, that Laterimeria, is a rhipidistian relative".

Coelacanth

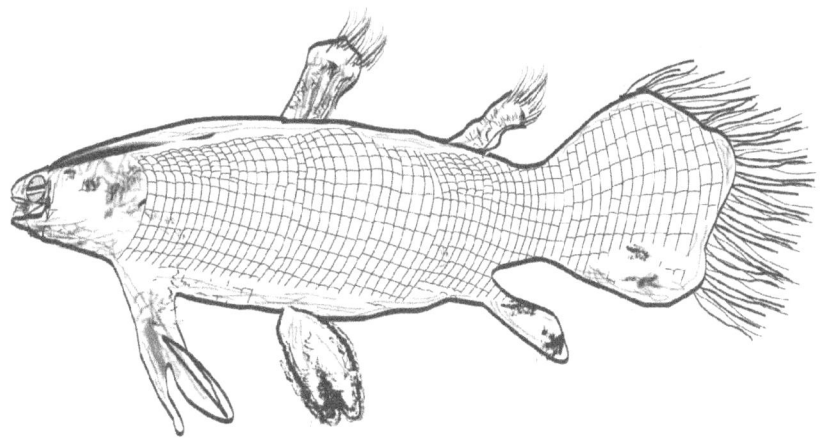

On examination, the Coelacanth was disappointing, much of its heart, intestine, brain is not what one would expect of a tetrapod ancestor, Barbara Stahl wrote;

"The modern coelacanth shows no evidence of having internal organs pre adapted for use in a terrestrial environment. The outpocketing of the gut serves as a lung in land animals is present but vestigial in Latimeria. The vein that drains it's wall returns blood not to the left side of the heart as it does in all Tetrapods" (Ref Micheal Denton, Evolution, A Theory In Crisis, page 179, 1996)

The transitional stages of the feather, feathered aerofoil or wing, avian flight had evolved? John Ostrom in "Bird Flight How Did It Begin? "page 46, 1979, gave the following accounts;

"Previous speculations on this question have produced two quite different scenarios. Stated very simply these are birds that began to fly "From the trees down" -or "from the ground up". The first is the favoured and logical arboreal theory. The second is the often ridiculed and less probable "Cursorial theory".

Gerhard Heilman, 'The Origin Of Birds" 1926, was an advocate for the arboreal theory. He attempted to explain that "frayed scale" aerofoil would work and transition to gliding to powered flight was feasible. His lack of mathematical knowledge of his reconstruction of pro-avis would lead to doubt that the wing/weight ratio would be insufficient for gliding, let alone flight. (Ref Micheal Denton, Evolution, A Theory In Crisis, page 205, 1996)

Glenn L. Jepsen 'Selection Orthogenesis and The Fossil Record' 1949 page 491.

Jepsen evolutionists believe that the bone may be older than the cartilage, that elasmobranchs may have developed from bony forms.
(Ref John Klotz, Genes Genesis and Evolution page 461)

The oldest of the bony fish is the Cheirolepis. It dates from the middle Devonian period of Great Britain, presumably a third branch of ostracoderms. Crossopterygians - lobe fins believed to have developed as a branch from primitive ostracoderms. The earliest Osteolepis from the middle of the Devonian period of Europe, a small shark-like fish.
(Ref John Klotz, Genes Genesis and Evolution page 461 1955)

Lungfish the first of these was the Dipterus appeared in the Devonian period. The Crossopterygians the first of them were the Osteolepis of the Middle Devonian period of Europe, a small shark - like fish believed to give rise to the Eustheropteron from

the upper Devonian period of Canada. Latimeria seven specimens is a crossopterygian.
(Ref John Klotz, Genes Genesis and Evolution page 466 1955)

Earliest of the amphibian fossils is from the Upper Devonian of East Greenland.

Jerry Coyne gave this account which he regarded as;

'One of the best examples of evolutionary transitions, was in the fossil records of whales; since we have a chronologically ordered series of fossils, perhaps a lineage of ancestors and descendents, showing their movement from land to water, showing their movement from land to water.'

In Coyne's statement in which he says;

'With the recently discovered fossil of a close relative of the whales, a racoon size animal called the Indohyus.living 48 million years ago. Probably very close to the whale ancestor looked alike.

Coyne also says;

Indohyus was not an ancestor of whales, but was almost certainly it's cousin'.

If we look into what Coyne is suggesting, then we have to look at a further 4 million years, 52 million years, we have a fossil of a skull of the wolf-like creature Pakicetus. Under examination the Pakicetus is more whale-like than Indohyus and it lived 4 million years before Indohyus, so this can contradict Coynes theory.

Micro-evolutionary changes are sometimes claimed to be macro-evolutionary. Lake Turkana showed that certain snails and bivalves (freshwater mollusks) changed substantially when the lake was isolated from other waters, but such changes stopped when the isolation ended. There is no evidence that such changes transgress the limits of micro-evolution. (Ref Colin Mitchell, Case for Creationism, pages 124-125, 1994)

Arthropods

The arthropods are regarded as the highest form of the invertebrates. Mollusks are in its equal. The earliest of the arthropods are the trilobites. They are found in the lower Cambrian rocks. They are sometimes known as "rock bugs". Each of their body segments have a pair of undifferentiated appendages. They are believed to be parapods of the annelids, but were joined. Their head was covered with a dorsal shield.

The arthropods also include lobsters' crabs' spiders.

Some evolutionists believe that the trilobites were ancestral to modern crustaceans. Most evolutionists believe that trilobites and crustaceans are parallel offshoots of a primitive pre-Cambrian annelid.

The mollusks are regarded as a peculiar branch of this stock. Trilobites, and other arthropods are regarded as progressive descendants of this stock. Mollusks developed a skeleton of lime. Trilobites then developed a skeleton of chitin.

It is believed Trilobites then gave rise to forms to primitive horse-shoe crabs, and scorpions. Crustaceans cast off their old skin as their bodies increase in size. Mollusks cannot do this. (Ref John Klotz, Genes Genesis and Evolution, pages 447-448)

Ostracoderms

Ostracoderms were from the vertebrate fishes from the Paleozoic period. They were found in the Ordivician and the Devonian period in Europe and N. America. They were divided in two groups: the heterostracans and celephalapids.

The name "Ostracoderm" means "shell-skin" and refers to the fact that these had a head and trunk covered with a hard bony shell or shield. They were long, sluggish, poor swimmers, they had a lob-sided tail for power. (Ref John Klotz, Genes Genesis and Evolution pages 459 to 460)

Cyclostomes

The Cyclostomes are the lampreys and hagfishes, and the gnathostomes being over 60,000 species.

The Ostracoderms are believed to have given rise to the Cyclostomes. They only have a cartilaginous skeleton, with no backbone. They are parasites and have caused problems for the fishing industry. (Ref John Klotz, Genes Genesis and Evolution page 460)

Elasmobranchs

Elasmobranchs are modern sharks that have a cartilaginous skeleton.

Another branch of Ostracoderms gave rise to modern elasmobranchs. These are modern sharks and rays. They have a cartilaginous skeleton. It is believed that the cartilage is older than the bone, as it has been found in highly developed forms than bones. Some evolutionists believe that the bone may be older than cartilage, J.R. Norman, A History of Fishes, 1949, page 124, comments on this. (Ref John Klotz, Genes, Genesis and Evolution page 461)

First Bony Fish

The oldest of the bony fish is the Cheirolepis, it dates from the Middle Devonian Period of Great Britain. It had developed from the third branch of the Ostracoderms. These early bone fish had lungs of the Devonian period (Ref John Klotz, Genes Genesis and Evolution page 461)

Crossopterygians

These are mainly lobed-finned fish, coelacanths. Porolepifoms and onychodontiforms were from the Devonian period.

It was on Dec 22 1938, a fisherman on the Chalumna Bank in the Indian ocean off the African Coast, A Blue Metal coloured fish about five feet long was caught. The fisherman took it to a scientist as the fish looked strange. The fish was recognised as being a Coelacanth of the Early Mesozoic Period.

It has been said that the chondrichthyans were an example of evolution from simple ray-finned fish to the lobed-finned crossopterygians. It was the development of the pectoral fin to the standard vertebrate arm pattern. It is believed that the osteolepiforms evolved to four legged-animals the tetrapods.

The oldest known Crossopterygians were from the Early Devonian period. It has been said that the pectoral fins were in development from the first ray fish that the propterygium was in first stage., Then the mesopterygium was the second stage. Then the metapterygium was in the third stage of the development. The Lungfish was an example of osteichthyes evolution, if this evolution is possible! This is if the lungfish was a descendant of the crossopterygian. Then it was suggested that the lungfish gave rise to the amphibians.

Latemeria Chalumanae is the definition of the Crossopterygian fish. From the Upper Silurian period were the Sarcopterygians these were bony fish that did not have cartilage. Then from the Upper Devonian period they split into two groups;

1./ Coelacanths

2./ Rhipidistia

Coelacanths are found in the oceans, and are Carboniferous, while the Rhipidistia was more used to freshwater, and were found near estuaries, mouths of rivers.

Supposed Extinct Forms Still Alive

Coelacanth fish - Latimeria Chalcumare a living specimen found in South Africa in 1937, believed to be extinct 50 to 120 million years. Another specimen was found in December 1952, and another in the Indian Ocean Madagascar in August 1953, 7 Latimerias were found.

(Ref Genes Genesis Evolution John Klotz, page 200, 1955)

Protozoa

Protozoa are simple one-celled organisms. These could not have existed without plants. Euglena was believed to be the link to plants and animals. The first of the true protozoa is believed to have a form similar to modern heliozoa or radiolaria.

Heliozoa are one-celled organisms surrounded by a gelatinous matrix - lattice like case. They have many radiating strands of protoplasm known as pseudopods "sun animalcules". They mainly live in freshwater. The radiolaria are similar to heliozoa. Their cytostome is separated into an inner and outer portion of the capsule. They have a skeleton of silica/strontium sulfate. They are marine and pelagic, living in the ocean. (Ref John Klotz, Genes, Genesis and Evolution page 436, 1955)

There have been reports of radiolaria in preCambrian rock. There is no real evidence they exist in Proterozoic and Archeozoic rocks. Cambrian rocks, the protozoa make up 0.4% of the fauna. Amoeba are only known from the late Paleozoic rocks of the Carboniferous period. (Ref John Klotz, Genes, Genesis and Evolution pages 437-438, 1955)

Amphibians

Evolutionists derive amphibians from the crossopterygians. (Ref Barrett - Hamilton, E.H. Herald, M.A.C. hinton "History of British Mammals" 1910, 1921.

It is believed that Crossopterygians is the Osteolepis from the Middle Devonian period of Europe. It was then believed it gave rise to the Eusthenopteron known from the Upper Devonian period from Canada. (Ref Genes Genesis and Evolution John Klotz 1955)

Amphibian Evolution

The earliest known amphibian fossils came from the Upper Devonian of eastern Greenland. They consist mainly of skulls. There were no limb bones with these skulls. Early crossopterygians developed fore and hind limbs strong enough for walking. (Ref Genes Genesis and Evolution John Klotz 1955)

Palynology

The real evidence has been suggested that from amoeba to man must lie in the geological record, this evidence mitigates against a history of phylogenetic developments.

Palynology is the study of pollen grains of plants. Pollen grains have outer walls called exine. There are two types, the monocolpate, and the tricoplate.

S. Leclerc of "Evidence of Vascular Plants in the Cambrian" 1956, he believed that the woody vascular plants were established. Leclerc however made differences of vegetation that were in the Lower Devonian to the Upper Devonian periods.

The Upper Devonian had ferns and related forms, as well as conifers and related forms and the Lower Devonian had semi-aquatic forms like psilophyte and lepidodendron forms. He considered that the Lower Devonian was present during the Middle Devonian, the Middle Devonian forms were present during the Lower Devonian.

A short amount of time, for the Lower Devonian flora to evolve into the Middle Devonian, has been indicated that would be contrary to evolutionary process. The Lower Devonian flora, perhaps existed in the Middle Devonian, but the flora has not been found as fossils. In the Middle Devonian period flora was found and in the Lower Devonian but again no fossils found.

Austin Clark "Animal Evolution 1928" wrote, "The fossil record does not support the tree of life, but presents the evolutionist the necessity of explaining the development of a whole forest of trees (polyphyletic evolution). Most early Paleozoic sedimentary rocks are marine, not continental. (Ref Walter E. Lammerts Why Not Creation, Pages 180 to 183)

Agassiz in his studies "Principles of Zoology" stated;

"The progress of beings on the surface of the earth. This progress consists in an increasing similarity to the living fauna,and among the vertebrates, especially in their resemblance to man. The fishes of the Paleozoic age are in no respect the ancestors of the reptiles of the Secondary age, nor does man descend from the mammals that preceded him in the Tertiary age. The link by which they are connected is of a higher and immaterial nature; and their connexions is to be sought in the view of the Creator himself........Man is the end towards which all the animal creation has tended, from the first appearance of the first Paleozoic fishes." (Ref Samuel Kinns P.H. D., F.R.A.S. The Harmony of the Bible and Science page 357, 1895)

Embryonic Relationships

This can be explained by the basis of recapitulation De Beer says the failure to recognize this principle of parallelism of increasing degrees of complexity was a grave error in the theory of recapitulation.

Many invertebrates excrete nitrogen in the form of ammonia. Fish and amphibians excrete at its urea. Birds excrete nitrogenous wastes as uric acid. The embryo bird first excretes ammonia then urea. As an adult it excretes uric acid. This seems to be a case for recapitulation.

Joseph Needham "The Biochemical Aspect of the Recapitulation Theory" 1930, he pointed out there is no evidence at all for recapitulation. He believes it represents an order of biochemical reactions. He said the production area by the chick embryo is by the arginine-arginase system, not identical with fish, and amphibia. (Ref John Klotz, Genes, Genesis and Evolution pages 152 -153)

Stebbins believes that in plants the growing tip (apical meristem) produces appendages of a more specialized type and develops late.

De Beer stated, the notochord develops to be destroyed by the vertebral column. This not being a result of evolutionary recapitulation but the notochord in undoubtedly formed during gastrulation.The cells later constitute the notochord being then able to form axial structures of the embryo, spinal cord, eyes, ears, muscles, kidneys.

De Beer also stated that of course evolution of species has diverged to an extent that only similarities appear and dissimilarities are lost. He believes that embryology cannot with any degree of certainty reconstruct ancestral types. He believes that embryology may give some indication of affinity. The descendant, he says, may be derived from a larval form of ancestor, and in such case the resemblance between the young form of the descendant and the young form of the ancestor may convey little or no information concerning the adult form of that ancestor.

De Beer 'Embryology and Evolution' page 60 this was his comment on the theory of Recapitulation;

'The failure to recognise this principle of parallelism of decreasing degrees of complexity was a grave error in the theory of Recapitulation'. (Ref Genes Genesis Evolution John Klotz page 156, 1955)

Walter Garstang "The Theory of Recapitulation A Critical Statement of the Biogenetic Law" 1922. He believed that the embryonic ancestor resembles the adult descendant. He believes that modern man resembles the young Neanderthal man or newborn ape, and that vertebrates have developed from larval echinoderms. Insects have developed from larval echinoderms.

Problems with Vertebrate Origins

The invertebrates, annelids and arthropods, have a ventral nerve cord. Their nerve cord is solid, their hearts are dorsal. The vertebrates have a dorsal nerve cord, their hearts are ventral. (Ref Genes Genesis and Evolution John Klotz 1955)

The vertebrates did not appear till the time of the highest Silurian beds (Ludlow), in which was found the oldest known fish, the Pteraspis.

Parallel Evolution

Some biologists believe that the evolution of chordates has paralleled the evolution of the invertebrates. The two groups are believed to have evolved in parallel paths. Animal life started in two forms, an invertebrate protozoan, and a vertebrate similar to Amphioxus. (Ref Genes Genesis and Evolution John Klotz 1955)

There are no primitive vertebrates found in fossils of early rock strata. No chordates in Cambrian rock. The first are not protochordates, but are vertebrates - fish, these are found in Silurian rock. (Ref John Klotz Genes, Genesis and Evolution, page 457)

Chordate Evolution

There has been no agreement as to which path has been taken. Some suggest the primitive chordates gave rise to Amphioxus. From Amphioxus, two types have been developed, the first of these became a side branch and developed into modern ascidians. These are primitive chordates that never develop the vertebral column found in vertebrates. The ascidians have a notochord and a nerve cord for larvae and are believed to represent a sort of degenerate type of evolution from Amphioxus.

The second type to develop from Amphioxus was the primitive fish type, similar to the ostracoderms. These gave rise to modern fish.

Another part of evolution of the vertebrates has been suggested that the basic chordates developing into primitive fish, such as the ostracoderms (as mentioned) Ostracoderms gave rise to Amphioxus and the related cephalochordates., which then gave rise to Ascidians. (Ref John Klotz, Genes Genesis and Evolution page 458)

Supposed Extinct Fossils

It was believed that Dawn Redwood, Metasequoia glyptostroboides had been extinct for 20 million years. In 1944, its existence was reported by a chinese forester, Tsang Wang he found it in the province of Szechwan in central China. A grove of these trees were found in the Shueisha valley.

A land animal, coelacanth fish, Latimeria chalumnae. A living specimen was taken off the coast of Africa in 1937. It was believed to be extinct from 50 to 120 million years. Another specimen was taken in December 1952, off Comore Island in the Indian Ocean near Madagascar. (Ref John Klotz, Genes, Genesis and Evolution page 200)

Blum believes that oxygen has always been present in the atmosphere, and what we have now did not come from the photosynthesis of CO_2. he did believe that there was more CO_2 present.

D.M. Raup 'Field Museum of Natural History' 1979. His comments on Darwin;

'Well we are now about 120 years after Darwin and the knowledge of the fossil record has been greatly expanded. We have a quarter of a million fossil species but the situation hasn't changed much. The record of evolution is still surprisingly jerky, and, ironically, we have fewer examples of evolutionary transition than we had in Darwin's time. By this I mean that some of the classic cases of Darwinian change in the fossil record, such as the evolution of the horse in North America, have had to be discarded or modified as the result of more detailed information what appeared to be a nice, simple progression when relatively few data were available, now appears to be much more complex and much less gradualistic.' (Ref Oliver Barclay, Creation and Evolution, page 149, 1985)

Numerous reports have appeared of the discovery of fossils of alleged single-celled, microscopic, soft-bodied bacteria and algae in pre-Cambrian rocks. Most geologists date the Cambrian period as the beginning about 600 million years ago stretching through 80-100 million years, while the preCambrian Period refers to Sedimentary rocks believed to be older than the Cambrian.

If the complex invertebrates found in the Cambrian evolved from a single-celled ancestor, the record of the transition should be found in the preCambrian rocks. If the fossils of microscopic single-celled , soft-bodied bacteria can be found, there should be no problem at all in finding fossils of transitional forms between these and complex invertebrates of the Cambrian. Not a single transitional form, however between single-celled organisms and the complex Cambrian animals has ever been found. (Ref Oliver Barclay, Creation and Evolution, page 150, 1985)

The idea that the vertebrates were derived from the invertebrates is purely an assumption that cannot be documented from the fossil record. The transitional fish to amphibia is supposed to have required about 30 million years about. Somewhere in the fossil record we should find transitional forms documenting the transition, for example, of fins feet and legs.

It was claimed that Archaeopteryx was a transition from reptile to bird, whereas it was classed as a bird. Articles have documented that Archaeopteryx had feathers identical to those of modern birds and that there is nothing in the structure of the pectoral girdle of Archaeopteryx that would preclude it's having been a powered flier. It has been suggested that the fossil of a modern type bird has been found in Upper Jurassic rocks, The same rocks in which Archaeopteryx is found. If this is confirmed, Archaeopteryx would be the ancestor of modern birds. (Ref Oliver Barclay, Creation and Evolution, page 154, 1985)

D.M. Raup 'Conflicts Between Darwin and Paleontology' Vol 50 page 25, 1980.

He spoke of the incompatibility of the fossil evidence.

Verna Wright says 'The fact that Raup speaks of the incompatibility of the fossil evidence and Darwin's theory, because of the 'incompleteness' of the fossil record, which today is almost unmanageable rich.'

So the fossil record is unmanageably rich!

He says that Duane Gish's book 'Evolution - The Fossils say No!, that 'Readers should consider carefully the evidence cited in that book'.

Fossil Record Incomplete

In the oldest of rocks, pre-Cambrian or Cambrian, the fossils being aquatic. First plants were algae on the basis of the remains. All animals, invertebrates spread over the most important phyla, like sponges, jellyfish, crustaceans, starfish, worms. It is found that all divisions of the animals were formed in the Cambrian period except vertebrates. The vertebrates appeared in the next or Ordovician period, depending on the evolution theory. In the early fossils, nearly all the phyla appear in rocks as fully formed.

If evolution is true, phyla should have evolved one from another in an increasing scheme of complexity and diversity. Fossils should connect with the phyla unmistakably. None of these were found (Ref Walter E. Lammerts Why Not Creation, page 344).

For more explanation on the evidence on the missing links;

G.G. Simpson "Genetics, Paleontology, and Evolution 1949" said, "The palaeontological evidence for discontinuity consists of the frequent sudden appearance of new groups in the fossil record, a suddenness common to all taxonomic levels and nearly universal at high levels. Since the record is, and must always remain, incomplete, such evidence can never prove the discontinuity to the original."

Oswald Spengler "The Decline of the West 1962" wrote this regarding the fossil record;

"There is no more conclusive refutation of Darwinism than that furnished by paleontology. Simple probability indicates that fossil boards can only be test samples. Each sample, then, should represent a different stage of evolution, and there ought to be merely "transitional" types, no definition, no species. Instead, we find perfectly stable and unaltered forms preserved through long ages, forms that have not been developed themselves on the fitness principle, but appear suddenly and at once in their definitive shape; that do not evolve towards better adaptation, but become rarer and finally disappear, while forms crop up again. What unfolds itself in ever-increasing richness of form is the great classes and kinds of beings which exist aboriginally and exist still, without transition types, in the grouping of today."

This seems a 9 out of 10 account on the weakness of evolutionary theory, and notice an excellent part of this quote "there ought to be merely 'transitional types' so fossils can represent a stage of evolution! Brilliant. Transitional types of fossils, not a single one ever to be found, or to put it succinctly ever existed!

Then there is another problem with the fossil record that is "skipping". Land snails in the Carboniferous period disappeared then reappeared in the Cretaceous period, then persisted into present times. Scorpions in the Upper Silurian disappeared to the Carboniferous. Spiders disappear after the Cretaceous,to reappear in the Tertiary period.

The shrimp, too the Anaspides, has not been found as any fossil in any rocks since the Carboniferous, though they appear in the mountain streams in Tasmania.

The coelacanth, Latimeria, which was supposed to be extinct in the Devonian period. From this Devonian period until today there has not been one fossil found, yet nine were found off the island of Madagascar in 1958.

Wyatt Durham "The Incompleteness of our Knowledge of the Fossils Record" pages 559 -565, 1962.

In his article;

'As many as two percent of all marine invertebrate species with hard skeletal components that have ever existed may be known as fossils' This would be assuming that ten to twenty species are genus.'

M.J.S. Rudwick "The Meaning of Fossils , Neal Watson Academic Publications pages 228, 239. 1972.

'They......were all aware of the intrinsic imperfections of the record of the whole groups of organisms, like insects, or never preserved at all. However, this did not affect their increasing confidence in the adequacy of the fossil record as evidence for the major outlines of the history of those groups which possessed readily fossilised skeletal parts'

(Ref Micheal Denton, Evolution, A Theory In Crisis, pages 190 to 191)

John Phillips a leading palaeontology, who gave a lecture at Cambridge 1860, Life On Earth, Its Origin and Succession;

'Most palaeontologists of the time would probably have agreed with him when he maintained that Darwin had grossly overstated the case for the imperfection of the fossil record'

Fossil Sequence

The lowest Palaeozoic sediments contain mainly bottom dwelling marine creatures; mammals appear in the late Mesozoic.

Fossil Record Fossil Preservation

Devonian fish fossils give the impression that a disaster must have suddenly destroyed vast shoals of fish, piling them one above another without damage to their skeletons, with every fin erect and intact.

The fossil record shows that some perished in the midst of their activities such as feeding or giving birth. Ref from H. Miller 'The Old Red Sandstone, 1870, made comment to this.

In some Carboniferous sediments a mixture of corals and crinoids suggests cataclysmic destruction, and similar features occur in Cretaceous rock.

For the lack of preCambrian fossils in Preston Cloud of "Pre-Metazoan Evolution and the Origins of the Metazoa" 1968, gave the following account;

'To such hypothesis, I will comment only that (1) the availability or lack of $CaCO3$ is not an explanation for distribution of fossils observed - carbonate rocks are abundant, both and above the Paleozoic - Precambrian boundary. The "Lipalian" gap does not exist; sequences of sedimentary rock transitional from Precambrian into Cambrian appear to be present in Australia, etc., The absence of Precambrian littoral and intertidal sediments invalid.... Precambrian sediments of ages and depths with a degree of fidelity would assure the preservation of tracks, trails, burrows of the afterdeath impressions of pelagic metazoan organisms if they had been present. A very long interval of pre skeletal metazoan seems unlikely. The 50 to 100MY preskelatal development represented by the Ediacaran is not out of the question. Brachiopods could hardly exist in context with a shell. (Ref Micheal Denton, Evolution A Theory In Crisis pages 187, 188, 1996).

On his own account Darwin said;

'The explanation lies, as I believe, in the extreme imperfection of the geological record'.

Thomas Schopf, ("Punctuated Equilibrium and Evolutionary Stasis" page 160, 1981) commented in Paleobiology;

"Note the case of the Order Multituberculata, the longest living mammalian order. It is considered to range from the middle Jurassic to the end of the Eocene, 160my duration. Stage by stage basis fossils of this order are known to occur in stages whose cumulative duration is only 87my. 54% of the duration of the order. 46% of the time Multituberulata existed, and there has not yet been discovered a record of the order anywhere in the world." (Ref Micheal Denton, Evolution, A Theory In Crisis, pages 188 to 189)

Of the Terrestrial vertebrates 79.1% have been found as fossils, birds which are poorly fossilized, the percentage rises to 87.8%.

Wyatt Durham "The Incompleteness of our Knowledge of the Fossils Record" pages 559 -565, 1962.

In his article;

'As many as two percent of all marine invertebrate species with hard skeletal components that has ever existed may be known as fossils' This would be assuming that ten to twenty species are genus.

M.J.S. Rudwick "The Meaning of Fossils , Neal Watson Academic Publications pages 228, 239. 1972.

'They......were all aware of the intrinsic imperfections of the record of the whole groups of organisms, like insects, or never preserved at all. However, this did not affect their increasing confidence in the adequacy of the fossil record as evidence for the major outlines of the history of those groups which possessed readily fossilised skeletal parts'.

(Ref Micheal Denton, Evolution, A Theory In Crisis, pages 190 to 191)

John Phillips a leading palaeontology, who gave a lecture at Cambridge 1860, Life On Earth, Its Origin and Succession;

'Most palaeontologists of the time would probably have agreed with him when he maintained that Darwin had grossly overstated the case for the imperfection of the fossil record'.

Darwin admitted that many of his contemporaries were not prepared to concede that the record was sufficiently imperfect to account for the gaps.

"That the geological record is imperfect all will admit; but that it is imperfect to the degree required by our theory, few will be inclined to admit." (Ref Micheal Denton, Evolution, A Theory In Crisis, page 191, 1996)

As the populations in geographical areas are very small, the chance of fossilization of transitional forms is low, Stephen J. Gould "The Panda's Thumb, page 184, 1980, said there are bound to be gaps between species;

"In any local area inhabited by ancestors, a descendant species should appear suddenly by migration from the peripheral region itself, we might find direct evidence of speciation, but such good fortune would be rare indeed because the event occurs so rapidly in such a small population. Thus, the fossil record is a faithful rendering of what evolutionary theory predicts."

(Ref Micheal Denton, Evolution, A Theory In Crisis, page 193, 1996).

Protozoa

Protozoa are simple one-celled organisms. These could not have existed without plants. Euglena was believed to be the link to plants and animals. The first of the true protozoa is believed to have a form similar to modern heliozoa or radiolaria.

Heliozoa are one-celled organisms surrounded by a gelatinous matrix - lattice like case. They have many radiating strands of protoplasm known as pseudopods ``sun animalcules". They mainly live in freshwater. The radiolaria are similar to heliozoa. Their cytostome is separated into an inner and outer portion of the capsule. They have a skeleton of silica/strontium sulfate. They are marine and pelagic, living in the ocean. (Ref John Klotz, Genes, Genesis and Evolution page 436)

There have been reports of radiolaria in preCambrian rock. There is no real evidence they exist in Proterozoic and Archeozoic rocks. Cambrian rocks, the protozoa make up 0.4% of the fauna. Amoeba are only known from the late Paleozoic rocks of the Carboniferous period. (Ref John Klotz, Genes, Genesis and Evolution pages 437-438.)

Sponge Evolution

Sponges have developed from a specialized type of protozoa called Choanoflagellate. These are flagellates that belong to the Euglena. Each of the single-celled individuals has a long lash, or flagellum surrounded by a funnel or delicate protoplasmic collar. Sponges are the main line for evolution.

The recognized metazoan species are the following;

Insects 500,000 - 750,000

Sponges 4,500

Coelenterates 9,000

Echinoderms 4,200

Annelids 7,600

Other worms 9,000

Molluscoids 3,300

Mollusks 80,000 -104,000

Crustacea 15,500

Myriapods 8,100

Arachnids 28,000

Vertebrates 40,000 - 70,000

James Valentine, of the University of California, "General Patterns of Metazoan Evolution" 1977, pages 27 to 57 his comments;

'There are numbers of both soft - bodied and skeletons fossils of the late Pre-Cambrian or Cambrian ages which are not assignable to living phyla, nor can any of them.'

There have been attempts to explain the mystifying absence of primitive transitional forms in the preCambrian rocks. One explanation was that before the Cambrian age aquatic animals did not possess shells or hard integuments or that they possessed shell-like structures so fragile that no traces have been found, because the calcium content of the sea was supposed to have been too low to permit the secretion of calcareous shells. Another explanation was that there was a long lapse of time, the "Liplalian gap" between the latest preCambrian rocks during which time no fossil bearing rocks were laid down. Another possibility was that there was an absence of intertidal and near shore littoral sediments laid down in pre-Cambrian rocks. (Ref Micheal Denton, Evolution, A Theory In Crisis, page 187, 1996)

Arthropods

The arthropods are regarded as the highest form of the invertebrates. Mollusks are in its equal. The earliest of the arthropods are the trilobites. They are found in the lower Cambrian rocks. They are sometimes known as "rock bugs". Each of their body segments have a pair of undifferentiated appendages. They are believed to be parapods of the annelids, but were joined. Their head was covered with a dorsal shield.

Some evolutionists believe that the trilobites were ancestral to modern crustaceans. Most evolutionists believe that trilobites and crustaceans are parallel offshoots of a primitive pre-Cambrian annelid.

The mollusks are regarded as a peculiar branch of this stock. Trilobites, and other arthropods are regarded as progressive descendants of this stock. Mollusks developed a skeleton of lime. Trilobites then developed a skeleton of chitin.

It is believed Trilobites then gave rise to forms to primitive horse-shoe crabs, and scorpions. Crustaceans cast off their old skin as their bodies increase in size. Mollusks cannot do this. (Ref John Klotz, Genes Genesis and Evolution, pages 447-448)

Origin of Insects

It was thought that trilobites gave rise to insects. Many evolutionists believe that insects developed directly from the preCambrian annelid stock. De-Beer suggests they originated from the larvae of some myriapod forms of a retention of juvenile characters. (Ref Genes Genesis and Evolution John Klotz 1955)

R.J. Tillyard "The Biology of the Dragonfly, Cambridge University Press," page 215, 1917. Commented on the Dragonfly;

'The apparatus of the male Dragonfly is not homologous with any known organ in the Animal Kingdom; it is not derived from any pre-existing organ; and it's origin, therefore, is as complete a mystery as it well could be'. (Ref Micheal Denton, Evolution, A Theory In Crisis, page 220, 1996)

Eclectic Theory, Gregory says characteristics found in various invertebrate forms are eclectic. These features are not found in any single invertebrate form, but in several invertebrate forms

Agassiz, classified fishes by the following;

1./ The Placoids, (From broad plate), having an internal cartilaginous skeleton, were covered externally with armature plates, and points of bone.

2./ The Ganoids, (From Splendour) referring to the brilliant surface of their enamels, armour of enamelled bone, bony plates that lock into each other at their edges, like Sturgeon.

3./ The Ctenoid, (From a comb) Fishes covered with scales that of a horny substance and pectinated at the lower edges, like teeth of a comb, as in Perch.

4./ The Cycloids (From a circle) whose scales are like a continuous margin, like Salmon.

(Ref Samuel Kinns PH.D.,F.R.A.S. The Harmony of the Bible and Science, pages 263, 264, 1895)

Ostracoderms

The name "Ostracoderm" means "shell-skin" and refers to the fact that these had a head and trunk covered with a hard bony shell or shield. They were long, sluggish, poor swimmers, they had a lob-sided tail for power. (Ref John Klotz, Genes Genesis and Evolution pages 459 to 460)

Cyclostomes

The Ostracoderms are believed to have given rise to the Cyclostomes. They only have a cartilaginous skeleton, with no backbone. They are parasites and have caused problems for the fishing industry.

(Ref John Klotz, Genes Genesis and Evolution page 460)

Elasmobranchs

Another branch of Ostracoderms gave rise to modern elasmobranchs. These are modern sharks and rays. They have a cartilaginous skeleton. It is believed that the cartilage is older than the bone, as it has been found in highly developed forms than bones. Some evolutionists believe that the bone may be older than cartilage, J.R. Norman, A History of Fishes, 1949, page 124, comments on this.

(Ref John Klotz, Genes, Genesis and Evolution page 461)

Crossopterygians

Crossopterygians are believed to have risen from primitive ostracoderms. The earliest being the Osteolepis from the Middle of the Devonian period of Europe. It was a small shark like predaceous fish. It was covered with ganoid scales.

Fish Evolution

The first of these were the armoured holostean ganoids, in which the skeleton is fully ossified.

The second was a derivative from the palaeoniscoid were the Amiidae.

The third was a derivative from the paleoiscoids were the teleost or modern fish, the leptolepis which were probably plankton. Over time they became more bony and less cartilage.

Whales the last shore dwelling ancestor was the Sinonyx said to have existed 60 million years ago.

The transition from land animals to whales in this 60 million years was;

1./ Sinonyx, hyena like animal

2./Indohyus

3./Ambulocetus

4./Rodhocetus

5./Basilosaurus

6./Dourado

7./Humped back whale

Jawless Fish

a./ Ostracoderms

b./Cyclostomes

Placoderms. Well-defined jaws, well armed. Extinct since Permian times.

Eugnathostomates

a./ Elasmobranchs - sharks and rays

b./ Choanata - fish which originally had paired lungs

1./ Dipnoans - modern lungfish

2./Crossopterygii

Bony Fish paleonscoids

1./Teleostei- gar pike

2./Amodei - modern bowfin

3./ Sturgeons and Spoonbills

4./Teleostei - modern fish

(Ref Genes Genesis and Evolution John Klotz 1955)

The "telome theory" is a popular theoretical plan for deriving the vascular plants (plants with food and water conducting systems) from simple ancestors. This theory suggests that the branched leafless plants of the Silurian and the Devonian were working models of vascular plant ancestors. (Ref Walter E. Lammerts Why Not Creation 1969, page 231).

There are two problems with the "telome theory".

1./ The leafless and much branched are not simple.

2./ In the fossil strata, they appear to be already complex in their tissue structure, since they have been found to possess conducting cells, stomata, guard cells, spores, etc.,These plants were in fossil rocks with no previous lineage. Evolutionists believe these plants came from green algae, there are no known ancestors for them. The leaves were supposed to have formed as branch systems, condensed and fused by evolution. In rocks of the same fossil layer Devonian, plants that are fan shaped are present.

Aldanophyton antiguissiumum is a fossil plant specimen that shoots. This plant occurs in the Siberian Middle-Cambrian rock and is supposedly older than Rhynia species.

Groups of plants are independent entities as back as the fossil record, this is the reason that some evolution's accept the polyphyletic view of land plant origin.

Stratigraphic studies show fern fossils, the coenopterids appear mostly in the Carboniferous after more complex protopteridae, which show back up to the Devonian.(Ref Walter E. Lammerts Why Not Creation page 233)

It has been suggested that seed ferns arose from the true ferns (fern-like plants without seeds). Some of the seed fern plants that are present in earlier records, than the true ferns, and for this reason evolutionists believe that ferns and seed ferns had an independent or polyphyletic origin. There is no evidence that the pteridosperms originated from true ferns. They appear in the Lower Carboniferous leaving no clues of ancestral history.

The cycadophytes (plants like the modern cycads) were a already well-defined set of groups when they first appeared in the Permian and Triassic layers, (Ref Walter E. Lammerts Why Not Creation, page 236)

Taxales which are evergreen shrubs like the Yew trees, are other groups, are the other gymnosperms, Delevoryas stated that the Taxales were of a distinct group of the Jurassic times. It has been noted that the genus Lycopodites, of the Paleozoic is like the Lycopodium or ground pine of today. Modern ginkgos, plants with fan-shape foliage, have been found in the Upper Devonian to present. (Ref Walter E. Lammerts Why Not Creation, page 237).

Arthur C. Custance in the Earth Before Man, and Paul Zimmerman, Darwin Evolution and Creation. Have both suggested that there is evidence of gaps with supposed ancestral trees. The arthrophytes, in higher layers such as the Calamites, (tree-like plants resembling "norse-tail" of today. It is believed that it had descended from the Lower, Middle Devonian period. (Ref Walter E. Lammerts, Why Not Creation, page 240).

Heribert Nilsson, stated "My attempts to demonstrate Evolution by an experiment carried on for more than 40 years, have completely failed. At least, I should be hardly accused of having started from a preconceived anti-evolutionary standpoint…. It may be firmly maintained that it is not possible to make a caricature of an evolution out of paleo-biological facts. Ths fossil material is now so complete that it has been possible to construct new classes, and the lack of transitional series cannot be explained as being due to the scarcity of material. The deficiencies are real but they will never be filled.

Bibliography

Walter E. Lammerts, Why Not Creation 1969.
Paul S.Johnson, Epiphany Studies in Scriptures Series 2 Creation 1969
Colin Mitchell, Case for Creation 1994
Donald Patten, Biblical Flood Ice Epoch
Robert E.D. Clarke, The Universe, Plan or Accident, 1961.
Samuel Kinns PH.D F.R.A.S. Harmony of the Bible with Science 1896
Christianus Huygens, Dutch Physicist 1670, 'The New Conjectures Concerning Planetary Worlds, Their Inhabitants and Productions'.
Michael Denton, microbiologist, 'Evolution A Theory In Crisis' 1996
H.Jeffreys, 'Nature Of The Earth' 1959
G.Gamow, 'The Creation of The Universe' 1955
A.D. Lovejoy, 'The Great Chain of Being' 1961
R.J.Cuffey, 'Palaeontologic Evidence and Organic Evolution' 1972.
R.Barclay, 'Creation and Evolution' 1987
Sir William Dawson 'Primitive Nan' 1874
T.D.Stewart. 'Origin and Evolution of Man' 1950
Le Gros Clark, 'The History of Primates' 1957
Henry Field, 'The Iranian Plateau Race' 1940
Franz Weidenreich, 'Apes Giants and Man' 1940

Ernst Albert Hooton 'Upon From The Ape' 1946

www.ingramcontent.com/pod-product-compliance
Lightning Source LLC
Chambersburg PA
CBHW071614080526
44588CB00010B/1135